THE PHILOSOPHY OF MODERN SONG

BOB DYLAN

SIMON & SCHUSTER

NEW YORK   LONDON   TORONTO   SYDNEY   NEW DELHI

Simon & Schuster
1230 Avenue of the Americas
New York, NY 10020

First Simon & Schuster hardcover edition November 2022

SIMON & SCHUSTER and colophon are registered trademarks of Simon & Schuster, Inc.

Design by Coco Shinomiya

Manufactured in the United States of America

1 3 5 7 9 10 8 6 4 2

Library of Congress Control Number: 2022937213

ISBN 978-1-4516-4870-6
ISBN 978-1-4516-4872-0 (ebook)

For
DOC POMUS

Special thanks to my fishing buddy Eddie Gorodetsky for all the input and excellent source material, Sean Manning, Jackie Seow, Sal and Jeremy the Hot Rod Kings, all the crew at Dunkin' Donuts, P.K. Ferguson ("no hard and fast rules here"), and Jonathan Karp for his unwavering enthusiasm, expert advice, and encouraging me to stick with this, who said all the right things at the right time when I needed to hear them.

TABLE OF CONTENTS

THE PHILOSOPHY OF MODERN SONG

Your life is unraveling. You came to the big city, and you found out things about yourself you didn't want to know, you've been on the dark side too long.

CHAPTER 1

DETROIT CITY
BOBBY BARE

Originally released as a single
(RCA Victor, 1963)
Written by Danny Dill and Mel Tillis

IN THIS SONG YOU'RE THE PRODIGAL SON.

You went to sleep last night in Detroit City. This morning you overslept, dreamt about white snow cotton fields, and had delusions about imaginary farmsteads. You've been speculating about your mother, having visions about your old pappy, making up stories about your brother, and idealizing your sister, and now you want to go home. Back to where things are more neighborly.

From the postcards and junk mail that you dashed off, everybody assumes you're a bigwig, that things are cool and beautiful, but they're not, and the disgrace of failure is overwhelming. Your life is unraveling. You came to the big city, and you found out things about yourself you didn't want to know, you've been on the dark side too long.

By day you make the jeeps and limousines and the gas guzzlers, and by night you make the cocktail lounges. Everywhere you go people treat you like you are dead, everywhere you go you uncover more lies—if only they could read between the lines they could figure it out, it wouldn't take much guess work.

You rode a train full of merchandise northbound, and you ended up in Detroit City looking for a pot of gold, one fruitless search after another, each one taking an unexpected bad turn, and you're exhausted—seems like you've been here your whole life, squandering opportunities, lost opportunities. Every day another daily dose of poison, what are you going to do?

You're going to take your foolish self-love and egotism and go back to what's familiar, back to the ones that'll stand by you, the ones that you left in the background. You want to go back home, you demand that of yourself. You've got a thirst and a hunger and a need, you got to get up and go, beat it, and push off. Time to say adios. You want to go home, where they'll embrace you and take you in. Nobody will ask you for an explanation. No one's going to pepper you with relentless questions. You're going back to where you can clear your life up, going back to people of understanding. The people who know you best.

★ ★

WHEN THIS SONG WAS WRITTEN, Detroit was a place

to run to; new jobs, new hopes, new opportunities. Cars came off the assembly lines and straight into our hearts. Since then, like many American cities, it has ridden a roller coaster between affluence and decline. It has recently emerged from years of ruin, only to find itself tested again. But people from Detroit, the home of Motown and Fortune Records, birthplace of Hank Ballard, Mitch Ryder, Jackie Wilson, Jack White, Iggy Pop, and the MC5, can tell—any setback is only temporary, which is why dreams like Bobby Bare's seem as real today as the day they were first sung. He's able to manufacture a completely fictitious life just by penning some letters back home.

What is it about lapsing into narration in a song that makes you think the singer is suddenly revealing the truth?

Bobby Bare first tried his hand at becoming a recording artist back in the 1950s, eventually signing with Capitol Records and releasing a couple of singles that went nowhere. Trying his luck as a songwriter, he wrote "The All American Boy" and did a demo for his friend Bill Parsons. Bill recorded a version, but the record company, Fraternity Records, decided to release the demo that Bare had recorded. A clerical error left Bill Parsons's name on the label, so Bobby Bare's first chart hit was under the name Bill Parsons. This was probably the first incident of identity theft in America.

This is not so much the song of a dreamer, but the song of someone who is caught up in a fantasy of the way things used to be. But the listener knows that it just doesn't exist. There is no mother, no dear old papa, sister, or brother. They are all either dead or gone. The girl that he's dreaming about long ago got married to a divorce attorney and she has three kids. Like thousands of others he left the farm, came to the big city to get ahead, and got lost. That's why this song works.

CHAPTER 2

PUMP IT UP
ELVIS COSTELLO

Originally released on the album *This Year's Model*

(Radar, 1978)

Written by Elvis Costello

THIS SONG SPEAKS NEW SPEAK. It's the song you sing when you've reached the boiling point. Tense and uneasy, comes with a discount—with a lot of give-a-way stuff. And you're going to extend that stuff till it ruptures and splits into a million pieces. You never look back you look forward, you've had a classical education, and some on the job training. You've learned to look into every loathsome nauseating face and expect nothing.

You live in a world of romance and rubble, and you roam the streets at all hours of the night. You've acquired things and brought people the goods.

It's not like you have a promising future. You're the alienated hero who's been taken for a ride by a quick-witted little hellcat, the hot-blooded sex starved wench that you depended on so much, who failed you. You thought she was heaven and life everlasting, but she was just strong willed and determined—turned you into a synthetic and unscrupulous person. Now you've come to the place where you're going to blow things up, puncture it, shoot it down.

This song is in full swing. The one-two punch, the uppercut, and the wallop, then get out quick and make tracks. You broke the commandments and cheated. Now you'll have to back down, capitulate and turn in your resignation.

What is it about you anyway? You want to boost everything up, exaggerate it, until you can grip it and fondle it.

Why does it all seem so crooked and hush hush?

Why all the trivial talk and yakety yak?

Why all the monotonous and lifeless music that plays inside your head?

And what about that little she goat that won't go away? You want to maim and mangle her. You want to see her in agony, and you want to blow this whole thing up until it's swollen, where you'll run your hands all over and squeeze it till it collapses.

This song is brainwashed, and comes to you with a lowdown dirty look, exaggerates and amplifies itself until you can flesh it out, and it suits your mood. This song has a lot of defects, but it knows how to conceal them all.

★ ★

ELVIS IS ONE OF THOSE GUYS WHOSE FANS

fall somewhere between the two poles of passion and precision. There are people who tick off the boxes of his life with the same obsession of someone completing a train schedule while others don't know anything beyond the fact that he sings a song that accompanied a particularly devastating breakup. Very seldom a cheery wedding song but plenty of breakup songs.

Knowing a singer's life story doesn't particularly help your understanding of a song. Frank Sinatra's feelings over Ava Gardner allegedly inform "I'm a Fool to Want You," but that's just trivia. It's what a song makes you feel about your own life that's important.

Elvis Costello and the Attractions were a better band than any of their contemporaries. Light years better. Elvis himself was a unique figure. Horn-rimmed glasses, quirky, pigeon-toed and intense. The only singer-guitarist in the band. You couldn't say that he didn't remind you of Buddy Holly. The Buddy stereotype. At least on the surface. Elvis had Harold Lloyd in his DNA as well. At the point of "Pump It Up," he obviously had been listening to Springsteen too much. But he also had a heavy dose of "Subterranean Home-sick Blues." "Pump It Up" is a quasi-stop-time tune with powerful rhetoric, and with all this, Elvis exuded nothing but high-level belligerence. He was belligerent in every way. Even down to the look of his eyes. A typical Englishman or Irishman, didn't matter how much squalor he was living in, always appeared in a suit and a tie.

Back then English people appeared in suits and ties no matter how poor they were. With this manner of dress every Englishman was equal. Unlike in the States, where people wore blue jeans and work boots and any type of attire, projecting conspicuous inequality. The Brits, if nothing else, had dignity and pride and they didn't dress like bums. Money or no money. The dress code equalized one and all in old Britain.

"Pump It Up" is intense and as well-groomed as can be. With tender hooks and dirty looks, heaven-sent propaganda and slander that you wouldn't understand. Torture her and talk to her, bought for her, temperature, was a rhyming scheme long before Biggie Smalls or Jay Z. Submission and transmission, pressure pin and other sin, just rattled through this song. It's relentless, as all of his songs from this period are. Trouble is, he exhausted people. Too much in his songs for anybody to actually land on. Too many thoughts, way too wordy. Too many ideas that just bang up against themselves. Here, however, it's all compacted into one long song. Elvis is hard edged with that belligerence that somehow he is able to streamline into his work. The songs are at top speed and this is among his very best. In time Elvis would prove he had a gigantic musical soul. Too big for this type of aggressive music to contain. He went all over the place and it was hard for an audience to get a fix on him.

From here he went on to play chamber music, write songs with Burt Bacharach, do country records, cover records, soul records, ballet and orchestral music. When you are writing songs with Burt Bacharach, you obviously don't give a fuck what people think. Elvis blows through all kinds of genres like they are not even there. "Pump It Up" is what gives him a license to do all these things.

CHAPTER 3

WITHOUT A SONG
PERRY COMO

Originally released as a single

(RCA Victor, 1951)

Music by Vincent Youmans

Lyrics by Billy Rose and Edward Eliscu

THIS SONG DOESN'T REALLY NAME the song that the world would be worse off if it never heard. It's a mystery. Elvis Presley quotes the first verse of this song as being representative of everything he believes. Most people first heard this song sung by Perry Como.

Perry Como was the anti–Rat Pack, like the anti-Frank; wouldn't be caught dead with a drink in his hand, and could out-sing anybody. His performance is just downright incredible. There is nothing small you can say about it. The orchestration alone can knock you off your feet.

Perry is also the anti–American Idol. He is anti–flavor of the week, anti–hot list and anti-bling. He was a Cadillac before the tail fins; a Colt .45, not a Glock; steak and potatoes, not California cuisine. Perry Como stands and delivers. No artifice, no forcing one syllable to spread itself thin across many notes.

WITHOUT A SONG
MUSIC BY
VINCENT YOUMANS
Lyrics by
WILLIAM ROSE &
EDWARD ELISCU
Sung by
LAWRENCE
TIBBETT
in The
PRODIGAL
With
ESTHER RALSTON
ROLAND YOUNG and
CLIFF EDWARDS
A HARRY POLLARD production
A Metro ~ Goldwyn ~ Mayer Picture
VINCENT YOUMANS, Inc., Music Publisher 67west 44th. Street, NEW YORK
Barbelle

He can afford to be unassuming because he has what it takes. A man with lightning in his pocket doesn't ever brag. He walks out onstage, cocks his head to better hear the band, stands in front of the audience and sings . . . and the people in front of him are transformed. Not by the clothes on his back or the drink in his glass, not by the last starlet he kissed or the car that he drives. But by the song that he sings. And without this song he has nothing, and this is the song he sings.

Perry Como lived in every moment of every song he sang. He didn't have to write the song to do it. He may have believed the songs more than some of the people that wrote them. When he stood and sang, he owned the song and he shared it and we believed every single word. What more could you want from an artist?

Without a song. Few songs become popular but the ones that do we can't seem to do without.

Get you away from the gangsters and psychopaths, this menagerie of wimps and yellow-bellies. You want to be emancipated from all the hokum.

CHAPTER 4

TAKE ME FROM THIS GARDEN OF EVIL

JIMMY WAGES

Recorded by Sun Records, 1956—unreleased

Written by Jimmy Wages

WHAT YOU'D LIKE TO SEE IS A NEIGHBORLY

face, a lovely charming face. Someone on the up and up, a straight shooter, ethical and fit. Someone in an attractive place, hospitable, a hole in the wall, a honky-tonk with home cooking. Nobody needs to be in a quick rush, no emphasis on speediness, everybody's going to measure their steps. Your little girl will support you; she waits on you hand and foot, and she sides with you at all times.

But you're in limbo, and you're shouting at anyone who'll listen, to take you out of this garden of evil. Get you away from the gangsters and psychopaths, this menagerie of wimps and yellow-bellies. You want to be emancipated from all the hokum. You don't want to daydream your life away, you want to get beyond the borderlands and you've been ruminating too long.

You've been suspended in midair, but now the stage is set, and you're going to go in any direction available, and get away from this hot house that has gone to the dogs. The one that represses you, you want to get away from this corrupt neck of the woods, as far away as possible from this debauchery. You want to ride on a chariot through the pillars of light, you got faith, you're fearless and undaunted, you're hanging tough and sick of being hog tied and being held back. You want to be flung into a distant realm where you'll be redeemed, and you'll go with anyone who'll escort you out of this jungle of baloney and everything fishy. Even if you have to dog paddle your way across the seven seas, you'll do it, and you can bet on that, put money on it. You overpower your fears and wipe them out, anything to get out of this garden of evil. This landscape of hatred and horror, this murky haze that fills you with disgust.

You want to be piggy backed into another dimension where your body and mind can be restored. If you stay here your dignity is at risk, you're one step away from becoming a spiritual monster, and that's a no-no.

You're appealing to someone, imploring someone to get you out of here. You're talking to yourself, hoping you don't go mad.

You've got to move across the threshold but be careful. You might have to put up a fight, and you don't want to get into it already defeated.

★ ★

NOTHING ARTIFICIAL ABOUT THIS SONG, nothing

manufactured or contrived about it. Nothing cosmetic or plastic here. This is the real deal and it's off the map. No racial bloodlines here. This song is no joke.

The guitar player sounds like Luther Perkins playing a Gibson Les Paul, instead of his usual Fender. In fact, it sounds exactly like the part Luther would play, so it could be him. This is a Sam Phillips record. Raw and fearless as anything Sam ever recorded.

The singer Jimmy Wages grew up with Elvis in Tupelo, Mississippi, lived on the same block, until Elvis moved away to Memphis when he was eight years old. You have to wonder, what if Elvis had stayed in Tupelo, and Jimmy Wages had moved away? Also, you have to wonder, what if Sam had sent Elvis over to Luther's house instead of to Scotty Moore's? Scotty and Bill would then have been backing up Johnny Cash, and Luther and Marshall Grant would have been playing with Elvis.

The story goes that Sam would record just about anybody who came through the door, anybody with something different about him, someone with character and soulful brilliance. But with a record like this, Sam probably knew he could only go so far. This was not a record for teenagers. Is this a record he could take over to his disc jockey friend Dewey Phillips at WHBQ and play it on his *Red Hot & Blue* show? Not likely.

This record presses the panic button. This record might be the first and only gospel rockabilly record. This is evil as the dictator, evil ruling the land, call it what you will. Jimmy sees the world for what it is. This is no peace in the valley. This is a garden of corporate lust, sexual greed, gratuitous cruelty, and commonplace insanity. Hypnotized masses of people, and dyed-in-the-wool assholes, and the singer wants to be delivered from it, who wouldn't.

He wants Justice and Chastity to come down from on high and take him away. The little girl is going to set his pace, somebody else is going to fight his duel. This is as raw-boned and country as it gets, a song Elvis could have recorded, and it takes Sister Rosetta Tharpe a step further.

CHAPTER 5

THERE STANDS THE GLASS
WEBB PIERCE

Originally released as a single

(Decca, 1953)

Written by Russ Hull, Mary Jean Shurtz, and Autry Greisham

THE GUY IN THIS SONG HAS QUITE a back story
and has a lot to answer for. It's hard to be on the losing end of a lost cause, a
lost enterprise, a cause with no object or purpose, unequivocally false from
start to finish, the man is in mental bondage. He must justify and vindicate
his entire being, he's been betrayed by politicians back home, forsaken and
double crossed. Stabbed in the back by legislators and members of his own
government. He doesn't recall ever having a soul, or if he did, it's long dead at
the bottom of a lake.

He fought like a savage, he stuck a bayonet into babies' bellies and gouged out
old men's eyes. He's been unfaithful to the human spirit and he's assassinated
priests. He lost his independence years ago. He's lived on rations and he's done
degenerate and demonic things. He plugs his head into nightly dreams, and
sees million-dollar wounds, purple hearts. He sees his ranks whittled down
piecemeal. He rounds up the elderly, women and children, torches their huts,

and turns his machine gun on them. He sees shadowy figures in black pajamas and conical hats. He sees a little boy two years old and he murders him, he sees his buddies slit a little girl open with a knife, strip off her clothes and rape her, then he shoots her with an automatic, his horny buddy.

He's back home now, shrapnel in his arms and legs—mosquito bites, he tells himself. He is standing in a crowded room, in the tavern on the green, and he looks around, he is surrounded by the enemy, it's zero hour.

This is a ritual celebration where he is being honored as a hero, he tells the waiter to fill his glass to the brim. This is it. This is the way it is. It could not, not have been any other way.

★ ★

WEBB MAY HAVE SUNG LIKE A CHURCHGOIN'

man, but he dressed for the honky-tonk stage. And the man who dressed him was a Ukrainian Jew named Nuta Kotlyarenko who came, like so many others, to the United States one step ahead of the pogroms of czarist Russia. Young Nuta bounced from job to job, trying his hand at boxing and acting, picking up a wife in Minnesota and traveling with her to New York in the early thirties, where they started a business making decorative foundation garments for showgirls.

Soon Nuta became Nudie and traded New York for Hollywood, where he made use of his skill sewing rhinestones onto dancers' panties and eventually emblazoned hillbilly stars with showstopping suits of lights that electrified fans from Nashville to Bakersfield. He put wagons on Porter Wagoner and spiderwebs on Webb Pierce. He covered Hank Williams in musical notes and Elvis Presley in gold lamé.

Like with many men who reinvent themselves, the details get a bit dodgy in places, but it appears that there was a little dust-up with the law about a drug-running charge, which resulted in a short jail stay. You can only imagine how amused Nudie must've been when Gram Parsons came in, all cannabis giggling and part of the generation that thought they invented drug use, and requested a drug-themed Nudie suit. Some folks to the right of "Okie from Muskogee" were surprised that Nudie was willing to make that suit but Nudie was nothing if not practical and as long as Gram's money was as green as his weed, he got himself a suit.

The thing Nudie loved more than money was country music. His store was a haven and hangout for the biggest names and there was a small stage where everyone got up to play. George Jones in his shirtsleeves waiting for a fitting by Manuel Cuevas—who Nudie stole when he was Sinatra's personal tailor and who only left when he divorced Nudie's daughter—borrowing an acoustic guitar to debut "The Grand Tour." Little Jimmy Dickens trying out material he was going to perform at the Opry that weekend. Local bands hoping to be heard by a big name and picked up as an opening act. And if no one else was there to play, Nudie taking center stage with his trademarked mismatched boots and ten-gallon yarmulke, plucking a tentative mandolin and singing the songs he loved.

Nudie dressed four US presidents and two Popes. Two Oscar winners have picked up their awards in Nudie suits and Neil Armstrong is buried in one.

Nudie loved Webb Pierce—the fifties flamboyant Pentecostal church singer whose powerful high tenor voice was as loud as the sequined suits he wore.

The star of this song is the empty bourbon glass, and it's built around the same kind of crack guitar sound as on a Hank Williams record, as well as the magical open-string, strummed chord.

CHAPTER 6

WILLY THE WANDERING GYPSY AND ME
BILLY JOE SHAVER

Originally released on the album *Old Five and Dimers Like Me*
(Monument, 1973)
Written by Billy Joe Shaver

THIS IS A RIDDLE OF A SONG, the further you go with it, the stranger it gets, seems to have ulterior motives. Kind of song you don't see coming until it's on you. It's not easy to get a fix on this song, nothing to point you in the right direction. There's you, and there's Willy and there's the wandering Gypsy. Maybe one, maybe two people or maybe three. The sure thing about Gypsies is that they travel in packs, tribes, and clans. Gypsies have home rule, been sticking together for centuries. Some historians say they came out of Egypt, the original Egyptians. Forced from their home country by African workers, who were imported to do the manual labor—who eventually overran the indigenous people. Gypsies never travel alone, they're self-sufficient, and they don't take honorary members. If Willy's a Gypsy, then he's an imposter.

This song has a philosophical point of view. Keep moving, it's better, let the train keep on rolling. It's better than drinking and crying in your beer. Let's go. Let's go forever. Let's go till the glacial age returns. Willy will play you for a sucker, for him it's always the morning after and you're a lackey. Willy would like you to abandon your long-suffering wife, heavy with child, leave her and go with him. Says if you stay here, you do it at your own risk. Come on let's go, let's get a head start. He wants you to give up your wife and not argue about it. You and Willy, the wise man, and the fool. You're on the road to nowhere, won't be tied down—the good old boy and his country cousin, sponging off the ladies, who'll give you all their womanhood, and do right by you. They're standing in line and opening their hearts.

Willy the bronc buster, he's going to ride in the big rodeo contest, and lay his hands on some big prize money. And you, you're going to hit the bottle and tag along. You refuse to be tied down. You don't listen to anybody, but everything gets in. You're toasting each other and telling each other jokes, both of you have been kicked in the groin, time and time again, and it still hurts.

You're traveling on the moonlight gravel.

Willy's the wild one, he's the barbarian, the escaped wanderer, more of a beast than he seems to be. But you both spring from the same fountainhead. Both him and you are completely out of it, made of the same stuff. Where you come from, nothing has a fixed price, nothing is final. You never give anybody what they want, but you know how to bait them.

There's three people in this song. There's Willy, there's the wandering Gypsy, and then there's you. However you slice it—guy crush, third wheel—you're standing proud and aloof. At your best you're Sancho Panza, at your worst you get left behind. You have to open up your eyes before it's too late.

CHAPTER 7

TUTTI FRUTTI
LITTLE RICHARD

Originally released as a single
(Specialty, 1955)
Written by Little Richard and Dorothy LaBostrie

A-WOP-BOP-A-LOO-BOP-A-WOP-BAM-BOOM. Little Richard was speaking in tongues across the airwaves long before anybody knew what was happening. He took speaking in tongues right out of the sweaty canvas tent and put it on the mainstream radio, even screamed like a holy preacher—which is what he was. Little Richard is the master of the double entendre. "Tutti Frutti" is a good example. A fruit, a male homosexual, and "tutti frutti" is "all fruit." It's also a sugary ice cream. A gal named Sue and a gal named Daisy and they're both transvestites. Did you ever see Elvis singing "Tutti Frutti" on *Ed Sullivan*? Does he know what he's singing about? Do you think Ed Sullivan knows? Do you think they both know? Of all the people who sang "Tutti Frutti," Pat Boone was probably the only one who knew what he was singing about. And Pat knows about speaking in tongues as well.

There's a lot of people in Little Richard's songs. All the stereotypes: Uncle John, Long Tall Sally, Mary and Jenny, Daisy, Sue, and Melinda. They are all slipping by in the shady world of sex and dreams and giving you a run for your money.

Little Richard was anything but little. He's saying that something is happening. The world's gonna fall apart. He's a preacher. "Tutti Frutti" is sounding the alarm.

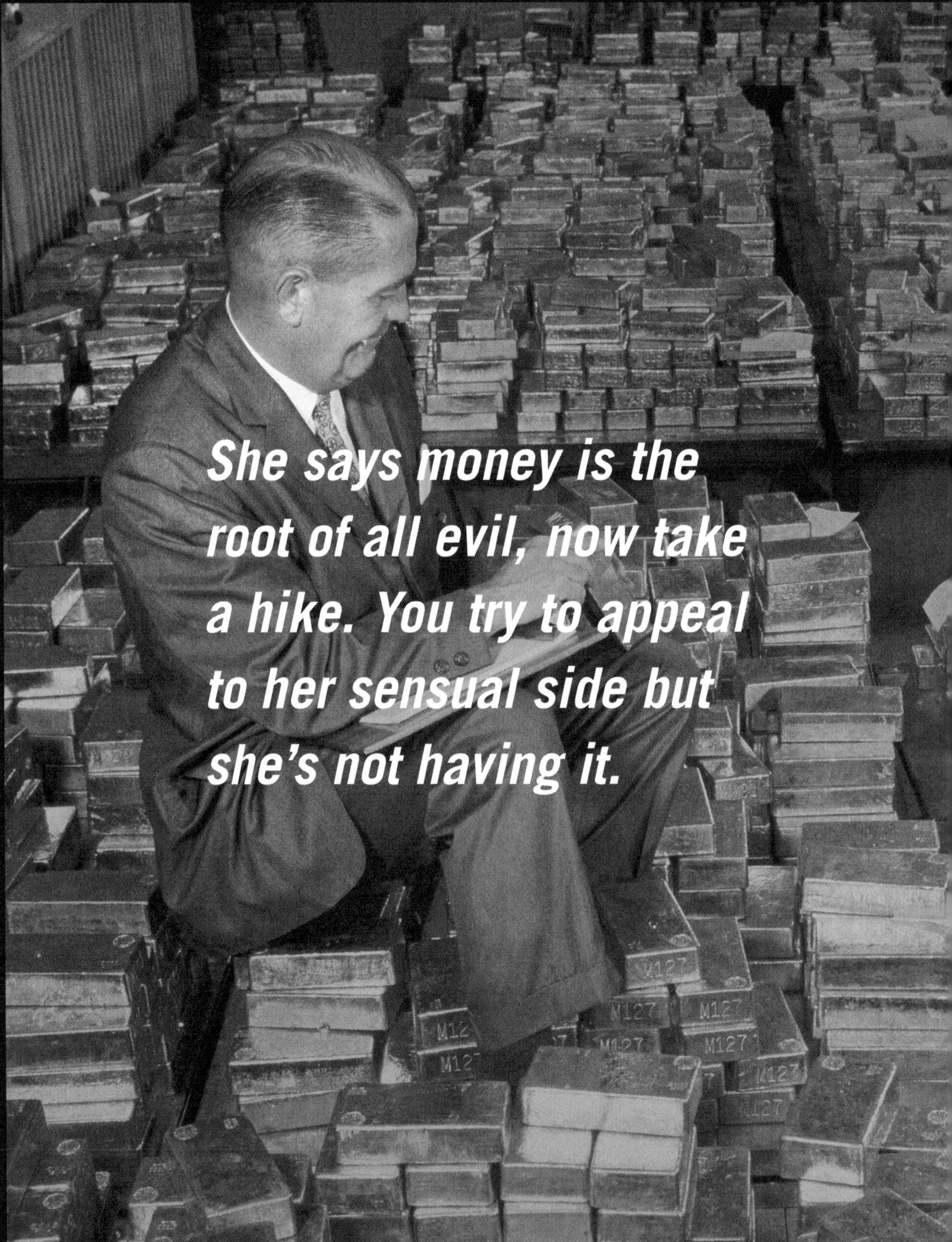

She says money is the root of all evil, now take a hike. You try to appeal to her sensual side but she's not having it.

CHAPTER 8

MONEY HONEY
ELVIS PRESLEY

Originally released on the album *Elvis Presley*
(RCA Victor, 1956)
Written by Jesse Stone

THIS MONEY THING IS DRIVING YOU up the wall, it's got you dragged out and spooked, it's a constant concern. The landlord's at your door and he's ringing the bell. Lots of space between the rings, and you're hoping he'll go away, like there's nobody home. You squint through the blinds, but he's got a keen eye and he sees you. The old scrooge has come for the rent money for the tenth time, and he wants it on the double, no more hanky-panky.

You give him the same old recitation, that times are tough, and your assets have been frozen, but you've got money coming in from a previous job. He doesn't go for any of it. You're on the defensive. The property owner is a doubting Thomas, the tight-fisted old penny pincher wants his money now. Pay up or vamos, if you want to stay chummy.

What do you do? You hoot and you howl, and you bark at the moon. You're beside yourself, you're fidgety. You call the hardest woman you know. Cream of the crop, coolest and the finest, your first and greatest love, you wake her up at 3:30 in the morning. She's irritated and fuming, and in a rage, wants to know why you called. You tell her you need a helping hand, and if she wants to stay on intimate terms, send you some cash.

She says look here mister lovey-dovey, you're too extravagant, you're high on drugs. I gave you money, but you gambled it away, now get lost. You say wait a minute now. Why are you being so combative? You're way off target. Don't be so small minded, you're being goofy. I thought we had a love pact, why do you want to shun me and leave me marooned. What's wrong with you anyway? I'm telling you, let's be amiable, and if you're not, I'm going to wrap this relationship up and terminate it. You're asking her for money. She says money is the root of all evil, now take a hike. You try to appeal to her sensual side but she's not having it. She's got another man, which infuriates you no end.

But no other man could step into your shoes, no other man can swap places with you. No other man would pinch-hit when it comes to her. How could it happen? I get it, she's not in love with you anyway, she is in love with the almighty dollar. Now you've learnt your lesson, and you see it clear. Used to be you only associated with extraordinary people, now they're all a dime a dozen, but you have to keep it in perspective. There's always someone better than you, and there's always someone better than him. You want to do things well. You know you can do things, but it's hard to do them well. You don't know what your problem is. The best things in life are free, but you prefer the worst. Maybe that's your problem.

★ ★

ART IS A DISAGREEMENT. Money is an agreement.

I like Caravaggio, you like Basquiat. We both like Frida Kahlo and Warhol leaves us cold. Art thrives with such spirited sparring. That's why there can be no such thing as a national art form. In the attempt, we can feel the sanding of the edges, the endeavor to include all opinions, the hope to not offend. It all too quickly turns to propaganda or rank commercialism.

Not that there's anything wrong with commercialism but like all things monetary, it's based on a leap of faith; more abstract than Frank Stella's geometrics. The only reason money is worth anything is because we agree it is. Like religion, these agreements can change according to country and culture, but those changes are merely cosmetic, usually only name and denomination. The basic tenets remain constant.

Money depends on the scarcity of what props it up for its value, but isn't that also an illusion? Rare and precious metals like diamonds are controlled by blood merchants who modulate their flow to keep the value at an acceptable level. And if gold is so rare, how are there enough gold bars to build a home for a family of two in Fort Knox alone?

It doesn't help that all things are constantly devalued. Before Gutenberg made type movable, only the wealthiest could afford books, and a Bible with tooled leather cover, gold-edged pages, and jewel-encrusted bindings was a symbol of not just piety but status, wealth, and taste. Within a few generations, the rabble were able to follow along in the hymnals from the cheap seats, forcing the wealthy to find another symbol to lord over the hoi polloi.

'Twas ever thus. The battle between the rich man and the poor man is fought on many battlefields, not all of them immediately obvious. Today the wealthy dress in sweatsuits and the homeless have iPhones. People with no discernible income buy flawless knockoff watches with one-letter misspellings to thwart copyright. And then wealthy people buy the same "Rulex" so their six-figure real watches won't get stolen when they are out at dinner.

SPECIAL ISSUE
LIFE
YOUR MONEY
HOW TO:
STRETCH IT
SPEND IT
SAVE IT
AND SURVIVE
WITHOUT IT
Money Doctor's Cure for Sick Budgets
Hidden Taxes: Sharper than a Serpent's Tooth
The Family Problem: Living on a Paycheck
A Family Making Its Biggest Buy: a House
A Millionaire's Tax Return
Osborn
APRIL 6 · 1962 · 20¢

The poor man sits in his broke-down economy car in the same traffic jam for an hour as the rich man in his luxury car. Sure, the seats may be plusher, the environment more controlled, but you're still stuck on the 405. One thing you can't buy is time. Professional hillbilly songwriter Bob Miller wrote a song about the inequities between the rich man and the poor man in life, but he found solace in the fact that both men would be equal when they took that final ride.

I had dinner a while back with a friend of mine who had recently lost his wife. He said something to me that I had to think about for a while. He said, "The only reason any of it means anything is because it ends." Unlike diamonds and gold, his time with his wife was truly finite and he had cherished every moment.

If you could live forever, it would be like money, shored up on an illusion, on a thing that was going to be there whether there was anything to back it up or not. In 2017 Venezuela had to issue a press release that it didn't have enough money to pay for its money. But you know what, Venezuela's still here. Because, ultimately, money doesn't matter. Nor do the things it can buy. Because no matter how many chairs you have, you only have one ass.

The landlord in "Money Honey" is a wastrel. Obviously, a man of means, a property owner, he goes himself to try and collect the rent from what appears to be a bad credit risk. The singer makes the landlord wait a long, long spell while he peeps through the blinds before finally asking the landlord what's on his mind. It turns out both men have money occupying their thoughts. It drives one to hide, the other to hunt him down.

By the end of the song, our narrator says he's learned his lesson, but what kind of lesson is it? The sun will shine, the wind will blow, women will come and go, but before he can appreciate the wonders of nature or swear love to any of the women, he must have money. As far as enlightenment goes, weak tea indeed.

I remember when this record came out. I knew people who thought the Drifters did it better. Other folks thought Elvis did it better. They could argue

all night about it. One thing they couldn't argue about was how much the record cost. That's another difference between money and art.

I wish I had a nickel for every song I knew about money, from Sarah Vaughan singing about pennies from heaven to Buddy Guy shouting the blues over a hundred-dollar bill. If you like greenbacks, Ray Charles has one song; the New Lost City Ramblers have another about greenback dollars. Berry Gordy built Motown on money, the Louvin Brothers wanted cash on the barrelhead, and Diddy knew it was all about the Benjamins. Charlie Rich sang "Easy Money," Eddie Money sang "Million Dollar Girl," and Johnny Cash could sing anything.

STEREO

THE WHO sings
MY GENERATION

including:
THE KIDS ARE ALRIGHT
INSTANT PARTY
OUT IN THE STREET
PLEASE, PLEASE, PLEASE

CHAPTER 9

MY GENERATION
THE WHO

Originally released as a single

(Decca, 1965)

Written by Pete Townshend

THIS IS A SONG THAT DOES NO FAVORS FOR

anyone, and casts doubt on everything.

In this song, people are trying to slap you around, slap you in the face, vilify you. They're rude and they slam you down, take cheap shots. They don't like you because you pull out all the stops and go for broke. You put your heart and soul into everything and shoot the works, because you got energy and strength and purpose. Because you're so inspired they put the whammy on, they're allergic to you, and they have hard feelings. Just your very presence repels them. They give you frosty looks and they've had enough of you, and there's a million others just like you, multiplying every day.

You're in an exclusive club, and you're advertising yourself. You're blabbing about your age group, of which you're a high-ranking member. You can't conceal your conceit, and you're snobbish and snooty about it. You're not trying to drop any big bombshell or cause a scandal, you're just waving a flag, and you don't want anyone to comprehend what you're saying or embrace it, or even try to take it all in. You're looking down your nose at society and you have no use for it. You're hoping to croak before senility sets in. You don't want to be ancient and decrepit, no thank you. I'll kick the bucket before that happens. You're looking at the world mortified by the hopelessness of it all.

In reality, you're an eighty-year-old man, being wheeled around in a home for the elderly, and the nurses are getting on your nerves. You say why don't you all just fade away. You're in your second childhood, can't get a word out without stumbling and dribbling. You haven't any aspirations to live in a fool's paradise, you're not looking forward to that, and you've got your fingers crossed that you don't. Knock on wood. You'll give up the ghost first.

You're talking about your generation, sermonizing, giving a discourse.

Straight talk, eyeball to eyeball.

★ ★

TODAY IT IS COMMONPLACE to stream a movie directly

to your phone. So, when you are watching Gloria Swanson as faded movie star Norma Desmond proclaim from the palm of your hand, "I am big, it's the pictures that got small," it contains layers of irony that writer/director Billy Wilder could never have imagined. Of course, someone streaming something to their phone is most likely watching something even shorter and faster paced on TikTok, certainly not anything in black and white with a running time of 110 minutes.

Every generation gets to pick and choose what they want from the generations that came before with the same arrogance and ego-driven self-importance that the previous generations had when they picked the bones of the ones before them. Pete Townshend was born in 1945, which puts him at the front end of the baby boomer generation, born right after the Second World War ended. The generation who fathered Pete and the rest of the boomers has been called the Greatest Generation—not a self-congratulatory term at all.

It might be helpful to take a moment and define terms just a bit. What exactly is a generation? Currently, the common definition is the period of time that the statistically largest portion of the population born within a thirty-year period is in control of the zeitgeist. Recently, we have entered a new phase, where anyone entering the age of twenty-two as of 2019 is now a member of Generation Z. While people make jokes about millennials, that group is now old news, as obsolete as all of the previous generations—the baby boomers, Gen X, the Fragile Generation, the Intermediates, the Neutrals, the Dependable, the Unshaken, and the Clean Slate.

Marlon Brando, like Elvis Presley, Little Richard, and the first wave of rockers, fell somewhere between the greatest generation ever and the baby boomers; too young to fight against the Nazis, too old to go to Woodstock. Yet when Brando replied, "Whaddya got?" when a local girl asked him what he was rebelling against in the movie *The Wild One*, it set the stage for the sixties and the rebellion against the picture-perfect prefab communities the boys came home from the war to build.

Like a lot of boomers, Pete seems to have a chip on his shoulder in this song. But he's not totally confident, he's somewhat back on his heels. There's a certain defensiveness. He knows people put him down just because he gets around. Perhaps he feels like he will never measure up or he knows they resent his generation's newly abundant leisure time. He wishes they would just disappear, fade away. He hopes he dies before he gets old and is replaced like he is replacing them. Pete can't even point the finger himself, he depends on his mouthpiece Roger to hurl the invective. That fear is perhaps the most honest thing about the song. We all rail at the previous generation but somehow know it's only a matter of time until we will become them ourselves.

Pete would probably be the first to tell you. He has a front-row seat for the history of his generation. He could read the picket signs against hatred and war. Well, that certainly ended that, thank you for your service. Each generation seems to have the arrogance of ignorance, opting to throw out what has gone before instead of building on the past. And they have no use for someone like Pete offering the wisdom of his experience, telling them what he has learned on the similar paths he has trod. And if he'd had the audacity to do so, there's every chance that person would have looked up at Pete and told him that he couldn't see him, he couldn't hear him.

And that gave Pete another idea.

CHAPTER 10

JESSE JAMES
HARRY McCLINTOCK

Originally released as a single

(Victor, 1928)

Traditional

BACK IN THE DAY WHEN JESSE JAMES prowled the countryside it was dangerous to be an outlaw. To be an outlaw meant that any citizen could legally shoot you and kill you on sight and claim the prize. An outlaw was a hunted man by society at large. He had to disguise himself, learn how to hide in plain sight, because anybody could shoot him. Absolutely anybody on the street. As a matter of fact, this is what did happen to Jesse James. It happened to many before him also and to some later. It was a very tough situation to be in. It's a little different today when being an outlaw is just a term. Country music has outlaws but nobody has any right to shoot these guys.

The rewards had to be pretty good seeing you'd become an outlaw yourself if you shot one of them. The modern days for these guys probably extended through the thirties with Pretty Boy Floyd and Bonnie and Clyde and Ma Barker's gang. In those days, if your face was in the post office on a wanted poster, anybody could shoot you. You had to be very careful.

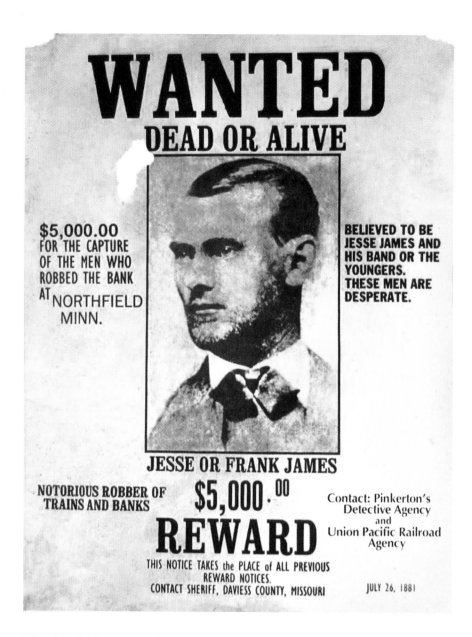

The English invented the outlaw. Anyone who shot a king's deer had a price on their head and anyone could kill them. It became a hobby for the English peasantry to bag one. In America, John Wilkes Booth was an outlaw. His picture was on wanted posters and anyone who found him could kill him and get the reward. In Booth's case, it was the authorities that found him and they received no reward because they were just doing their job. Another bounty left unclaimed.

If you harbor an outlaw, there is often a penalty for that too. It was the FBI who lobbied to keep outlaws out of the hands of citizens. It was too much competition, so they brought in laws to make it a crime to kill an outlaw if you didn't have a badge.

It was much easier to kill an outlaw than to bring him in, hunting the plains for high-paying quarry like some kind of bounty hunter romance story. You didn't want the hassle of having to haul an outlaw in alive because other citizens might kill him and hijack his corpse from you. Obviously, it was easier all around just to shoot him and be done with it. You can stick a dead body in a box and competing bounty hunters need not be the wiser.

Outlaws are different from common criminals. A common criminal can come in many guises. Criminals can wear badges, army uniforms, or even sit in the House of Representatives. They can be billionaires, corporate raiders or stockbroker analysts. Even medical doctors. But an outlaw has no protection from any group. He's cut off from society. No sponsors, no family to speak of, and where he goes, he goes unprotected. He is forced to be a rugged individual with no friends and no place to hide. He doesn't stand a chance of surviving. Jesse James sure didn't.

The outlaws of gangster rap and country music would not have fetched a high price back in the day. Their crimes are mostly those of braggadocio and wouldn't carry much on the open market. Conversely, Mafia kingpins and other white-collar criminals conduct their dirty business in towers far above the streets and are protected by levels of thugs who do their dirty work and lawyers who keep a distance from their names and their crimes. For that reason, they are criminals but not outlaws. Rap stars, country outlaws, hedge fund scammers, and mafiosos live in the lap of luxury while real gangsters like Jesse James hide in the shadows and fear death around every corner.

The thing about Jesse James is that his best friend became his worst enemy.

Now you're a wooden man, bloodless and cold, she came in first and racked off another win, came out on top, feather in her cap.

CHAPTER 11

POOR LITTLE FOOL
RICKY NELSON

Originally released as a single
(Imperial, 1958)
Written by Sharon Sheeley

IN THE PAST YOU ENTERTAINED YOURSELF

with other people's hearts, you stretched the rules. All you had to do was look at someone give them the eye and they wasted no time in coming to you, covered the ground in short time.

You went on a spree and left a trail of sensitive violated hearts, but that came to an end when you ran up against someone who buckled you, one on one, who made you fall to pieces and eat the dirt. You were brainless, no doubt about that. She played with you and teased you with her happy-go-lucky ways, she was easygoing and cheerful, unbothered. She fondled and stroked you, and with her baby blue peepers she enchanted you, she was a real knockout. She sized you up, she was captivating and shrewd and lousy with lies. Oh yeah, you were an absolute blockhead beyond a doubt.

She told you all kinds of things, how she adored you and would cherish you forever and she put you on a pedestal, she took charge over your inner being, never before had you ever exposed yourself to such an imposter.

Oh yeah, you were snowed most definitely.

Later on, when she was gone, you knew she'd been dishonest, told you many a tall story that you fell for, put up a nice front. Now you're a wooden man, bloodless and cold, she came in first and racked off another win, came out on top, feather in her cap. Poor little fool, yeah exactly.

You used to frolic and joke with other hearts like it was a contest, but if anybody ever thought that it would happen to you, they'd have to hold their breath. It would be a long wait, but it happened anyway. You got caught up in the senseless feeble-minded game, and you were consumed.

Now you're obsolete and out of date, and you're walking in the night down by the river, but the water's dead. You're moving one leg at a time. Another girl has got her hand on your shoulder, you're not always at your best.

★ ★

THE FOOL HAS GIVEN US MANY SONGS. Many

people do foolish things that are uncharacteristic of them. Maybe one small step in poor judgment can lead to a bad end. But we wouldn't call these people fools if they hadn't lived their life as one.

Ricky Nelson was no fool, he didn't walk around with no socks or feathers in his hair, he had all the right cards. High trump, low trump and all the picture cards. A ballad rockabilly singer with innocence and naivete on the surface, but a great depth beneath. Always at the forefront of new beginnings, improvising his place in the universe. You always knew what to expect.

There's lots of songs about fools. Aretha contemplates her place in a chain of fools, Hank Snow wonders how often there is a fool such as he, Paul McCartney contemplates one on the hill, Bobby Bland pities another while the Main Ingredient knows everybody plays one sometimes. The list goes on and on. Frankie Lymon wants to know why they fall in love, Jerry Garcia sang about a ship full of them, Elvis sang about their propensity to rush in where angels fear to tread and Anthony Newley didn't even know what kind of fool he was. And Ricky Nelson took his tuneful bit of self-realization, "Poor Little Fool," to the top of *Billboard*'s newly created Hot 100 in 1958. It was his first number one record, a height he would not reach again until 1961's "Travelin' Man."

But Ricky had long been poised for success. His parents' radio show, *The Adventures of Ozzie and Harriet*, based on the family's actual lives, had made the jump to television in 1952 after eight years. Ricky and his older brother, David, would become TV stars, and his long-playing album *Ricky* would make it to number one in 1957.

Ricky Nelson was a true all-American boy. He was a competitive sportsman, a star football player, a champion at tennis, and a high-wire trapeze artist. Even after breaking his hand during a practice, he wouldn't give up. By the time he graduated high school he'd become a starting member of the football squad. Ricky's dad, Ozzie, had been a starting quarterback at Rutgers before becoming a bandleader and sitcom star, so it ran in the family.

Ricky's parents, Ozzie and Harriet, were obviously the origins of Ricky's talents. Ozzie had been an orchestra leader in the thirties, and Harriet a big band singer.

There's an argument to be made that Ricky, even more than Elvis, was the true ambassador of rock and roll. Sure, when Elvis appeared on *Ed Sullivan*, everybody stopped and took notice, but Ricky was in your house every week. Along with guitarist James Burton and the rest of the band, Ricky made rock and roll part of the family. And not just for us but all over the world, magically transforming the image on a black and white television into the American dream. But mostly it was records that did it. Ricky was a part of the generation that had Buddy Holly, Little Richard, Chuck Berry, Gene Vincent, Fats Domino, and others, that made people from all nations, including commie countries, fall in love with America.

But Ricky wasn't one to let the grass grow under his feet, and in 1959 he gave the big screen a try, appearing alongside heavy hitters John Wayne and Dean Martin in *Rio Bravo*, a western directed by Howard Hawks. Ricky brought the same cool emotional detachment to the role of Colorado Ryan that he brought to his songs, emulating his father's laconic singing style. As opposed to many of his contemporaries who allowed themselves to get overheated, he maintained a steady hand as counterpoint to the emotion of the moment, to great effect. One wonders what his portrayal of some of the other roles of the time that he was offered, such as Stanley Kowalski in *A Streetcar Named Desire* or Lonesome Rhodes in *A Face in the Crowd*, would have been like. But a weekly television program and the demands of a recording career were already spreading him too thin, so we never got to see his interpretation.

And within a few years, the wheel turned as it always does, and they tried to relegate Ricky to the oldies circuit. Ricky wasn't having it. In 1971, Richard Nader tried to book Ricky for a rock and roll oldies show. Ricky agreed to appear on two conditions. They had to call the event the Rock and Roll Spectacular and he had to be billed as Rick, not Ricky, Nelson. He got them to change his name and the name of the event. None of this was known when Ricky played the Garden that night.

Bo Diddley, Chuck Berry, the Coasters, Bobby Rydell, a bunch of others. They were all good, did their hits. Rick was the only one out there trying to do new material. Oh, he did a couple of familiar songs. But he also did some of his newer songs. People booed.

Later he wrote a song about it, called "Garden Party," and took that song into the top ten. The people who came and saw him again didn't even recognize themselves in that song.

CHAPTER 12

PANCHO AND LEFTY
WILLIE NELSON
AND MERLE HAGGARD

Originally released on the album *Pancho & Lefty*

(Epic, 1983)

Written by Townes Van Zandt

A BIG PART OF SONGWRITING, like all writing, is editing—distilling thought down to essentials. Novice writers often hide behind filigree. In many cases the artistry is in what is unsaid. As the old saying goes, an iceberg moves gracefully because most of it is beneath the surface. That said, it is prescient that John Townes Van Zandt dropped his most prosaic given name early in life, whittling his identity down to an unforgettable run of syllables.

Born a square peg into the round hole of a wealthy family, Townes tried to fit in and become a lawyer like his dad. A love of Elvis Presley and various intoxicants derailed those plans. Lifelong battles with depression and addiction turned him inward and squeezed out dark hardscrabble songs from the depths of his sadness. Diagnosed with manic depression, Townes was shocked with both electricity and massive dosages of insulin. The treatments destroyed portions of his memories, which most likely is what gives his songs such a skeletal detached feel.

School and the military had no place for a shocked and broken poetic soul, and dreams of Elvis Presley were replaced by a love for the sadder songs of Hank Williams. He drifted and he drank. Texas was full of musicians to watch and learn from. Guy Clark, Gatemouth Brown, Jerry Jeff Walker, Butch Hancock, Doc Watson, Lightnin' Hopkins, Mickey Newbury, and Willie Nelson. Newbury brought him to Nashville, where he introduced him to Cowboy Jack Clement, a man who knew extreme behavior, having already produced Jerry Lee Lewis. This began a prolific, tumultuous, and ultimately disastrous chapter in Townes's life, culminating in lawsuits, accusations, and erased master tapes.

One way to measure a songwriter is to look at the singers who sing their songs. Townes has had some of the best—Neil Young, John Prine, Norah Jones, Gillian Welch, Robert Plant, Garth Brooks, Emmylou Harris, and hundreds of others. Another way to measure a songwriter is, are their songs still being sung? Townes's are. Every night—in small clubs, in lonely bedrooms, and wherever the brokenhearted watch the shadows grow long.

The worst thing about a song like "Pancho and Lefty" is that it put enough money in Townes's pocket for him to poison himself. He died on New Year's Day. Just as his idol Hank Williams had forty-four years earlier.

"Pancho and Lefty" is an epic panoramic tale, beautifully sung and beautifully produced, featuring two of the most iconic singers in the modern era. Willie Nelson could, as they say, sing the phone book and make you weep—he could also write the phone book, and Merle is pretty much the same.

Willie, in his pre-performing days, happened to be a door-to-door Bible salesman, and if his soulful vocal delivery is any indication of his personal magnetism and up-front honesty, then he must be responsible for half the Bibles in America. A bandito tale with two central figures—one, a swashbuckling

pistol-slapping big-sombreroed revolutionary, Pancho, and the other, a laid-back honey-voiced honky-tonk hero, Lefty. They're on the road to nowhere in the deserts of old Mexico. Pancho's got a horse as fast as a NASCAR racer, and Lefty can't sing the blues because he's been screwed up in the mouth by something either Pancho or the Federales did. He can't even talk, let alone sing. He drops out of sight, and ends up on the low side of Cleveland, in a fleabag hotel, on a lost-weekend trip, with thirty pieces of silver and a pistol to blow out his brains.

Pancho is a mama's boy, totally undisciplined and self-centered. He's always been encouraged to speak out about things that he's ignorant of. Pancho and Lefty are a match made in heaven but neither of them have found their true mate in life.

The underclass (the Honest World), the downtrodden peasants, are scared shitless of the ruthless Pancho. He squeezes them for all they're worth, and makes them suffer. Lefty is some kind of backstabber. Both these guys are nonconformist thieves. The aristocratic establishment, the upper-class land-owners, are too strong for them, and the lower classes have nothing much worth stealing, so they attack the middle class, taking advantage of and exploiting their false values, materialism, hypocrisy, and insecurities.

Pancho is also supplying the alcohol, drugs, and sex for them. Pancho's the man. Eventually he violates some kind of agreement with the Federales and his end is automatic. In another life Pancho would've been in the bullring and Lefty on the Ryman country music stage.

Pancho and Lefty. Two reflections of each other. Neither of these guys thought about how to make a successful exit.

CHAPTER 13

THE PRETENDER
JACKSON BROWNE

Originally released on the album *The Pretender*

(Asylum/Elektra, 1976)

Written by Jackson Browne

THIS SONG IS ARGUABLY ONE of Jackson Browne's greatest songs, from the album *The Pretender*. The Platters sang of the Great Pretender back in 1955, but like many things even pretenders got devalued between the fifties and the seventies.

★ ★

THE PRETENDER IS A MENACE to both church and society. Old age doesn't occur to him, and he has a rabid curiosity for the opposite sex. He is self-aggrandizing, and ever surrendering to the third person. The pretender is someone who has sold himself for a tiny little bit of the American dream. He's an ice-cream vendor, a drunk on a bender, a moneylender, and he could have been a contender, the pretender has drawing power.

He's on the move, he's always going to California. The pretender doubles down on everything, side steps what he doesn't like, and is good at getting himself out of his own way. He is slippery, he'll booze you up and strap you down, and he'll kill you with slogans. The pretender doesn't stand in the chow line, he packs his own snacks, holds down a job, goes home and settles down, goes to sleep, and gets up in the morning and does it again for an encore, his life is a broken record and he's got all the answers. For him love is dangerous work, and his success depends on being someone he's not.

He's trapped in the lesser world, the world of the legal tender, where sirens sing and the church bells ring, and the morning light streams in. The all-knowing light, the illuminating light, the light that's so bright it makes him blind as a bat. He's in for the long haul, caught between the hogwash and the filth—the no nothing and the no not what—he's the old pro looking for another war to fight—caught up in the machine of corruption, no regard for the things that come too quickly, he can't stand them. What he appreciates are the things that take him a long time to get, the things that make his life complete. The burdens of others will weigh him down, and so does his longing for love.

He's strolling in the moonlight, promenading down the boulevard, never lingers at a red light, doesn't want to be fossilized or turned into a mummy. He's cruising in the twilight, where the air is chilled and biting, where lovers find everything funny and chuckle and giggle, top it all off by engaging in great battles, tearing at the world, and mutilating everything in sight, brawling and getting into dogfights. He sees it all, dark glasses on his face to hide his eyes. But there are no eyes, no heart or soul, only empty pits, and a voracious sex appetite.

Last night he listened to jazz on the radio, Mingus, Brubeck and Monk, and fell asleep at another traffic light, wondering about utopia, a land he's heard about in a dream. He's thinking that someday he'll find everything that's been mislaid or left behind, that someday he'll find a girl that'll show him what giggling really means, and then he'll make love till he's exhausted, till all his power is gone, till his manhood is nonexistent—then he'll get up and do it again. He's already decided that. He's going to be out to lunch, a real dumbbell, and he's going to go all out for money. He's going to buy everything in every window display and get everything he sees in a commercial ad. Whatever it is, he's going to buy it, whatever the flyer says. He's going to be single minded and believe in everything that's profitable, everything he spends his dough on. He's turned over a new leaf, the street is his, and here he comes.

He was a youngster once, underdeveloped but fierce and hard as nails, but he capitulated, he raised the white flag. He thought his love could grapple with anybody, but it couldn't. If you want to say a prayer for the pretender, say it but be careful. Something might rub him the wrong way. The pretender doesn't want anything to be ordinary. He couldn't express it any clearer.

CHAPTER 14

MACK THE KNIFE
BOBBY DARIN

Originally released on the album *That's All*
(ATCO, 1959)
Music by Kurt Weill
Lyrics by Bertolt Brecht

IF YOU WERE AN ITALIAN KID growing up on the East

Coast in forties or fifties America, you most likely wanted to be Frank Sinatra. You inhabited him, you lived and breathed him—everything about him, the way he dressed, the way he sang, the way the girls flocked to his side and swooned. Bobby Darin would have had to have fallen under that spell. But whereas Sinatra just about invented the Roman Catholic Church, Darin was merely an altar boy. Frank had the strongest foundation any character could have. His father had been a bantamweight boxer and his mother was a skilled dealmaker and politically connected. Darin, on other hand, didn't know who his father was and thought his mother was his sister. He had absolutely no foundation and had to stand for himself alone. Whereas Sinatra was inclusive on every level, Darin would have had to have felt like rejected riffraff.

This song is from the German play *The Threepenny Opera*. Not really an opera, but more like a play with songs. The flip side being *Porgy and Bess*, which is thought of as an opera too, at least by George Gershwin. It was not really an opera either but rather just a simple story of a couple of people with songs scattered through it. But both of these so-called operas have unusual characters. Sportin' Life and Mingo, Strawberry Woman, Crab Man, Scipio, and others. The same kind of offbeat names appear in *The Threepenny Opera*: Polly Peachum, Tiger Brown, Filch, and Mack the Knife, among others. *Porgy and Bess* takes place on Catfish Row, a play that glorifies the pimp, the prostitute, the drug dealer, and murder in general. *The Threepenny Opera* does pretty much the same thing, only on a more sinister level. It's also a world of thieves, pickpockets, and drug runners. A world of small-time petty criminals, sneak thieves, gangster pimps, pickpockets, cigar-puffing killers—the subculture society that Hitlerism put an end to. And one of its songs is, of course, "Mack the Knife."

Bobby Darin broke through on the national scene with his teenage hit "Splish Splash," a monkey of a song, where his finger popping and crooning style was put to good use in the rock and roll domain. Were there similarities between him and Frank? Maybe. You would have to think so. But Darin was heading for a dead end and Frank would just go on and on. Darin could have been a movie star too, and he was to some degree, being a fine actor in his own right. But the parts had already come and gone. Frank could embody characters in movies like *Suddenly*, *The Joker Is Wild*, *The Manchurian Candidate*, and others. Darin could probably have played those roles too, but they were gone and he had to settle for useless parts in oddball movies.

Darin played in Vegas also, but it's hard to imagine him having a Rat Pack. If he did, you'd have to wonder who would be in it. Ben E. King? Wayne Newton? Robert Blake? Tuesday Weld? You can only dream. The most telling, weird combination, though, would have to be Frank's campaigning for John Kennedy and actually seeing him into the White House and singing at his inaugural ball, while Darin could only come up with his relentless campaigning for the martyred president's younger brother Bobby. John Kennedy actually did become president, but Bobby Kennedy was shot down before he could get there. Both Sinatra and Darin were shaken to the core. Their disillusionment would be all too similar. There are other similarities, too, but it's only in the metaphysical world that you'll find them.

"Mack the Knife" keeps on modulating till you think it will go through the roof. It's a murderous ballad, and Darin's performance is as good as and probably better than anybody's. He was at his height here. He would go on and try to follow Frank's formula but it was impossible—the world could only stand one Frank. Nobody could follow that road. Not Tony, not Dean, and certainly not Bobby Darin.

"Mack the Knife" is that dark road.

CHAPTER 15

WHIFFENPOOF SONG BING CROSBY

Originally released as a single
(Decca, 1947)
Music by Tod B. Galloway
Lyrics by Meade Minnigerode and George S. Pomeroy

THIS SONG IS THE GRINNING SKULL. An in-crowd song, a song with a pedigree, a song in the Social Register. Not meant for the middle class to understand—seems to house a deep dark secret. From the tables down at Mory's to the mysterious Louie and the dear old Temple Bar. Words of wisdom for those in the know. It paraphrases Kipling and lists a couple of songs no one's ever heard. A lot of bones and skeletons in this song. Even the word Whiffenpoof is a word to dispel spirits, and the melody is ancient—the last gasp, the beginning of the end. This is a song sung by dues-paying members of the inner circle.

Most people, nowadays, don't even know that they know the song. Whiffenpoof is just an alien word to them. But start singing "We're poor little lambs who have lost our way" and you pretty much guarantee that they will reply,

"Baa! Baa! Baa!" Bing sings this so straight, not a wink or bit of irony, that you think it must have deeper meaning.

Gentlemen rankers off on a spree, doomed from here to eternity. This song belongs to everybody, the fraternal order, the political machine, the silent majority, and the wealth of nations. It's predetermined, ordained, and comes right out of the book of Fate. Terrifying and hopeless. Guaranteed to keep your spirits up. It's standoffish and inaccessible—a Cabalistic song with a coded message. Sing it and it becomes entirely yours.

CHAPTER 16

YOU DON'T KNOW ME
EDDY ARNOLD

Originally released as a single
(RCA Victor, 1956)
Written by Eddy Arnold and Cindy Walker

YOU'RE NOT GOOD AT CHEWING THE FAT, and you don't want anybody putting words in your mouth, so you don't say anything. You can't go any further in the conversation—you're deadlocked with nothing to add.

You've got a great yearning and a hunger, a mad crush on someone, but she doesn't know you. She thinks she knows you well but she's wrong, she's always gotten the wrong impression. How could she know you? How could she know your wild dreams, your fantasies, nightmares and innermost thoughts, all the things you forbid her to know. It's just not possible.

How do you expect her to know you, she's not your alter ego or your double, to her you're just a patron, an associate, or a well-wisher, and that's all you've ever been.

She says goodbye a hundred times over, it doesn't matter that she says goodbye—what does matter is the way she says it. And she says it like someone

2

who doesn't know you. Why would she want to know you, you're a loner and scared stiff, you don't know anything about creating love, the kind that's manufactured and hyped up. You don't have the skill or the knowhow. You don't know how to pucker up and be sweet. By every indication, she has a soft spot for you, but it shakes you up and terrifies you, so there's no possibility of connecting up. You're not going to go out on a limb or lay yourself open.

The center of your entire being is aching and twitching because of her, and now of all things, you have to watch her walk away with the lucky bloke who holds all the aces, it's not easy. You don't want all of her love, just a little bit.

A little bit at a time, consistently—day and night spaced out over years. That's all you ask. To you she's larger than life, to her you're not even breathing. Your life is cursed.

★ ★

EDDY ARNOLD GREW UP ON A FARM, but he also

worked in the mortuary field. He was managed by Colonel Tom Parker, who eventually dubbed him "the Mortician Plowboy"—not even Solomon Burke could call himself that.

You don't call someone sitting on a tractor a plowboy. All this was done against Eddy Arnold's will. Colonel Tom Parker loved giving his clients nicknames. Much later in his career he gave Elvis Presley the title "the Hillbilly Cat," and Johnny Cash "the Big River Boy," and Hank Snow "the Singing Ranger."

A serial killer would sing this song. The lyrics kind of point toward that. Serial killers have a strangely formal sense of language and might refer to sex as the art of making love. Sting could have written this instead of "Every Breath You Take." He's watching her with another lucky guy. Not knowing where this happens makes you think that this could be happening totally inside the guy's head, at least until he picks up that knife.

Then it's the cold hard facts of life.

You're trying to act the way others want you to act, but it's a struggle. Sharp objects keep flying by. You're trying hard to absorb it all and keep your head above water.

CHAPTER 17

BALL OF CONFUSION
THE TEMPTATIONS

Originally released as a single

(Gordy, 1970)

Written by Norman Whitfield and Barrett Strong

IN THIS SONG EVERYTHING GOES OFF TRACK.

The Earth's terrestrial axis seems to have tilted a bit, and radical climate changes are threatening the planet. Chaos everywhere—prejudice and death, starvation, destruction. It's rolling like a ball and you're packed inside of it. These are turbulent times, and the sons of dogs are roaming the streets. Anarchy breaking out. The air is full of poison and the whole city is disorganized, none of the parts are in place. Your money doesn't buy you anything, or influence anybody. You're walking unsteady, get going they say, and you're marching along, confiding in the great Googa Mooga, your personal deity.

The hostility and disorder are like a horrible dream, you feel singled out and closed off. The topsy-turvy issues of the day have got you rattled, you can't describe what you're witnessing—and you're incapable of proving anything, and even if you could nobody's listening. Everything is iffy and unsafe. You're smack dab in the middle of it, you're an easy mark, and you keep appealing to the great Googa Mooga begging him for an escape route.

Things are tense, you quarrel with everybody. Blood running in the streets, earthquakes on the next block, women getting raped on the corner, spaceships taking off. Nothing fastened down. A new form of oppression every day. You're trying to act the way others want you to act, but it's a struggle. Sharp objects keep flying by. You're trying hard to absorb it all and keep your head above water. You used to have high hopes, high aspirations, you wanted to cure the insane, and practice abstinence. You wanted to be a lawyer for the poor, and now you can't find those thoughts, these are the facts of life.

The boss politician too, the old baby kisser who got your vote. He promised he'd set you free, but he turned coward and ran for the hills, brushed you off and gave you the cold shoulder. Everything's rotten and tainted, even your punch-drunk brother, he keeps talking about love, but what's that to you?

The more you think about it, the less sure you know what it means.

Kids too, they've developed too fast, they've got their heads above the trees, and they're easy targets. You're mystified, can't get any peace of mind, everything around you is disintegrating, and you're as far away as can be from normal life. You're telling this to the great Googa Mooga, telling him all, and that you're running for your life.

The new Beatles record intoxicates you—but you've no idea what you heard.

The atmosphere around you is exploding into pieces. More brutality more bloodshed, mob rule patrolling the streets. It's grossing you out and making your flesh crawl. Sonny and Cher are in your ear as well, and the beat doesn't stop. Besides that, your wallet is missing.

The Middle East is on fire, and a flood just knocked out a whole chunk of a city block. You just passed a magnificent funeral, and you took your own sweet time in passing by. You had nowhere to go and your equilibrium was off, there's fear in the air, a horrible funk that's giving you the jitters. A weird ectoplasm drifting up from the sewers is turning your stomach. What else could be wrong?

The city inspectors are after you for breaking the law, someone's informed on you. Bill collectors are chasing you down for money, your expenses are through the roof. You're demoralized and embarrassed, and now they want you to check your gun. You keep calling out to the great Googa Mooga, trying to communicate. You ask for wisdom from the ancient sages.

It's the same thing over and over, every ten seconds another news flash, another scandal, more headlines, more news commentators and they're giving you the creeps. Everything is spoilt dirty, everything you touch on. Everyone's rocking your boat, and they all seem to have a defect of one kind or another.

The public servants have failed you, and you're being asked for donations for another giveaway program. It's a jungle out there, and things are becoming unrecognizable. You're exhausted from all this, and you need something that's going to bring you around. You search for a safe place, a sanctuary, and you think maybe you'll go live with the Indians. You look for a secret passage to take you there. You wanted to be in on everything and now you are, you're right in the thick of it.

But then again, things might not be so simple, you may be hallucinating, making too much of it all, blowing everything out of proportion. You just might be a difficult person to get along with. This is a song where the singer has speculated long enough, and now he's ready to act. This is a song about the human condition, and rules don't apply.

★ ★

WHAT A DIFFERENCE TEN YEARS MAKES.

A decade earlier, Barrett Strong was the first Motown artist singing the ultimate song of greed with the self-penned "Money (That's What I Want)." Then in 1970, along with Norman Whitfield, he's written one of the few non-embarrassing songs of social awareness, which even manages to give a shout-out to the group that covered his first hit and made him a lot of money.

This might be the apex of everything that Barrett Strong and Norman Whitfield wrote. And they wrote a ton of great things: "I Heard It Through the Grapevine," "I Wish It Would Rain," "Cloud Nine," "Runaway Child, Running Wild," "Too Busy Thinking About My Baby," "I Can't Get Next to You," "War," "Just My Imagination," "Smiling Faces Sometimes," "Papa Was a Rolling Stone."

Writing a song like this can be deceptively easy. First you assemble a laundry list of things people hate. For the most part, people are not going to like war, starvation, death, prejudice and the destruction of the environment. Then there's the trap of easy rhymes. Revolution/evolution/air pollution. Segregation/demonstration. John Lennon got away with it by using his cheeky sense of humor to create a postmodern campfire song all about bag-ism and shag-ism. But in less sure hands one might as well write about the periodic table of elements with built-in rhymes about calcium, chromium and lithium.

Somehow, Barrett and Whitfield manage to avoid those pitfalls and many others even as they invoke then-topical songs like "Eve of Destruction" and "Indian Reservation." What sells "Ball of Confusion" is commitment.

You can see the pattern to their type of writing. Social issues, human nature issues—they could hide what they were trying to say and say it anyway. Usually songwriters write a few bad songs, if not many. But these guys don't seem to have ever written one. Everything they wrote is meaningful and true to life. It's the way things really are. They saw it and told it, relentlessly. They look into the darkness and shine the light. And then they move on and shine the light into a different darkness. But it's always darkness because you can't shine a light into the light. They're not preachers. The song is like an old radio show, where you could just imagine what you're listening to. And it made for a stronger experience. There's no way you could televise this song, it just wouldn't fit on a screen.

"Ball of Confusion" is pre-rap. If you're just walking around drunk and carefree, this song will sure sober you up. The reality of this song is that it's just as true now as the day it was recorded. There's also different musical interludes, like in a Roy Orbison song. Different voices singing different parts. But serious statements, unlike the Coasters, who might do a similar thing with only foolish talk. We need to hear this song again and again. It could have been written yesterday. Air pollution, revolution, gun control, more taxes, humiliation, obligation to our nation, vote for me I'll set you free. And the most current, rap on, brother, rap on. Nobody's interested in learning. Only safe place to live is on an Indian reservation. City inspectors, bill collectors, population out of hand. Everything let loose. Ten people talking at once. It's all right there. And the Temptations are the perfect group to pull it off, along with their great band.

A few years back, Motown released the Temptations' vocal recordings of their hits, including this one, stripped of the backing tracks. As beautiful and powerful as those backing tracks are, it is wonderful to hear the Tempts gathered around the microphone, a link to old-school doo-wop, harmonies delivered with real-time precision addressing the super-real problems of the day. A record is so much better when you can believe it.

Plus, Stevie Wonder plays harmonica here.

STAR

detective

CASES

DELL

25c

A LITTLE
LOVE...
A LITTLE
POISON

CHAPTER 18

POISON LOVE
JOHNNIE AND JACK

Released as a single
(RCA Victor, 1950)
Written by Mrs. Elmer Laird

THEY SING LIKE BROTHERS, but they weren't. Like the Bailes Brothers. Like the Stanley Brothers, like the Everly Brothers. But somehow these guys managed to transcend all that and sing like the brothers they were meant to be. They sing like one person. And they sing everything. They could sing rumbas and rock and roll and rhythm and blues and doo-wop and even country bluegrass. They were way into eclecticism long before Nashville recognized it. They sang like living breathing fire.

Johnnie and Jack ought to be in the Country Music Hall of Fame, but they're not. Obviously too radical for whatever is called country music. They've been passed up in favor of Barbara Mandrell and George Strait and the Statler Brothers. Evidently, Johnnie and Jack are not country enough. But they are actually country and more. They are closer to rockabilly, closer to rock and roll, so anyway, they shouldn't feel slighted. Gene Vincent's not in the Country Music Hall of Fame either. And neither is Warren Smith or Billy Lee

Riley. Johnnie and Jack are too outside for mainstream country. They should be in the Rock & Roll Hall of Fame too but they're not—even in the Rhythm & Blues Hall of Fame. They are not in there either. But they deserve to be in all the halls of fame, because they are innovators—innovators on the highest level—and don't jump through hoops for anybody.

The problem with halls of fame is that they celebrate sanitized versions of raw life. Country music finds itself in the church on Sunday morning because it spent Saturday night in a back-alley knife fight and trying to convince the barmaid to hike her skirt up around her hips. Without the dynamic tension of the guilt over the bacchanal, it becomes either joyless proselytizing or empty-headed carousing.

Rock and roll went from being a brick through the window to the status quo—from actual leather-jacketed greaseballs making rockabilly records to Kiss belt buckles sold in mall stores, to Thug Life press-on tattoos. The music gets marginalized as the bean counters constantly recalibrate the risk-to-reward ratio of public taste.

"Poison Love" is illicit love. Contrary to what most people think, when you pay money for sex, that's about the cheapest price there is. Complex relationships come with a high price. Better to go to a whorehouse or a bordello. It's not perfect love, but it's less problematic. You're not gonna come away singing about poison love. You get what you pay for (if you're lucky) and you walk away untarnished, unhurt. Nothing that's gonna drag you down. As they say in Australia, no worries. Poison love, that's the worst. That'll kill you. Lotta people out there who can't live without a daily dose of it.

Sailing towards your life—
your final destination.
You're checking your
compass, your almanac
and your horoscope.

CHAPTER 19

BEYOND THE SEA
BOBBY DARIN

Originally released as a single
(Atlantic, 1958)
Written by Jack Lawrence and Charles Trenet

IN THIS SONG YOUR HAPPINESS LIES beyond the wide sea, and to get there you have to cross the great unknown.

You're going out of bounds and you're into the briny deep—navigating by the stars, measuring longitudes and latitudes. You're the captain and you're sailing towards your nerve center, who is waiting in the coastlands upon the rich and rosy beach. She's waiting for you there, biding her time, sitting tight—she's on the lookout for you, checking out every ship. The clipper ships, the schooners and sloops. Onwards and onwards you go sailing over the bounding main, and off into the wild blue yonder. Sailing towards your life—your final destination. You're checking your compass, your almanac and your horoscope. The entire hemisphere is right there at your command, right there in your field of vision.

This is a good day if there ever was one. Round the clock, day and night, the breezes belong to you—all the waves are your friends. You're going over to the

far side, above and beyond, going off limits. You've been knocking about on this voyage since forever, riding on the crest of a high rippling wave, heading for a place you never heard of. You're the skipper.

Soon the fair winds blow you into the harbor, and you see the port lights. Soon you'll be approaching and coming up. You'll hit town and weigh anchor, and she's standing on the shores of everlasting gold. Soon you'll be shut off from the world, linked up everlasting. On top of each other, you'll kiss and embrace, every day from now on, a jolly holiday. Wonderfully brilliant and true to form. You see everything from the proper angle, you've returned to where you came from. No more casting off into a distant galaxy. No more cruising off into supernatural darkness. Never again you'll go sailing, you lay it all down and pull the shade. You quit while you're ahead.

★ ★

THIS IS A FRENCH SONG, originally written by Charles

Trenet, pretty much untranslatable. It's about the sea and all the allegory that it represents. Bobby Darin could sound like anybody and sing any style. He was more flexible than anyone of his time. He could be Harry Belafonte. He could be Elvis. He could be Dion, he could be a calypso singer, he could be a blue-grass singer or a folk singer. He was a rhythm and blues singer. The guy was everybody if anybody. But here's the thing about chameleons, if you don't watch them changing colors they just look like an ordinary lizard. Their uniqueness lies in their transformative nature. So, more fairly, Bobby Darin was more than a chameleon, for each of his guises he inhabited with verve and gusto and even in repose he just about vibrated with talent.

Perhaps he threw himself into every performance because he didn't expect to live long enough to have to hold anything in reserve. Even though he died tragically young, heart weakened by rheumatic fever, he lived longer than doctors ever expected him to. Every song was sung as if it might be the last one he would ever sing. But that doesn't explain the multiple personas.

Maybe that was because he had doubts about who he was. Like Eric Clapton, Jack Nicholson, and a surprisingly large number of others, Bobby lived in a household with a centrally placed lie. The woman he was brought up to believe was his sister was actually his mother, impregnated at a young age outside of wedlock, hidden away as she came to term and raised with the child as a sibling. The loving mother he believed he had was actually his grandmother. That would be reason enough to go into show business.

Some people create new lives to hide their past. Bobby knew that sometimes the past was nothing more than an illusion and you might just as well keep making stuff up.

Here, Bobby is as much of a swinger as he was in "Mack the Knife" but it fits him better. He doesn't feel like he is trying to fit into an older man's clothes. He doesn't start at full speed as he does on "Mack." Here, the band

eggs him on and the yearning of the first chorus gives way to the razzamatazz of finger pops and grunts that are imitated in a thousand karaoke bars every night. The drummer kicks his ass uphill at every turnaround.

His phrasing, especially on a pop ballad like this, is the driving wheel of the production. Time and time again he'll slip the first few words of a line upstairs into the end of the previous line. He's very subtle and you don't realize he's doing this. But if he sang songs like this straight, it probably wouldn't reach you. He's playful. He's a playful melodist and he doesn't need words. He keeps it simple even when he's singing about nothing. The sea, the air, the mountains, the flowers. It all floats. It never touches the ground.

CHAPTER 20

ON THE ROAD AGAIN
WILLIE NELSON

Originally released on the album *Honeysuckle Rose*
(Columbia, 1980)
Written by Willie Nelson

A SONG OF A TRAVELING BANDIT. A plunderer. The joy of moving, not staying anywhere. 'Cause they don't pay you to stay. They pay you to move. This is an update of the iconic beat generation masterpiece *On the Road*, by Jack Kerouac. On the road in this song means traveling by state-of-the-art tour bus: flat-screen TV, full-out bar, queen-sized bed in the back, a few extra bunks that are a world unto themselves, kitchen facilities, and leather booths, a shower and sometimes a steam bath. This is as good as the road gets. You never really go anywhere, you just stay in your bus, go out and perform for a few hours and move on. It's the way traveling bands hit the road. Like the Van Morrison song "Hard Nose the Highway." But Van travels by plane, so maybe he wouldn't know, but he's surely been told.

This song feels like the movement of the road. The way it feels on a bus, definitely not a sedan or an ambulance. When you're on the road, you're living the life you love. Making music with your friends, and earning a living. It's a happy song. Not one downer phrase in it. You could sing it anywhere—in a state fair or Radio City Music Hall. Commonality is its theme. It's kind of a religious hoedown.

On the other hand, you could just as easily construct a nightmarish song on the same subject full of the bumps in the road and tiny discomforts and indignities piled upon the weary traveler.

There could be verses about broken heat vents on the bus, sirens outside hotel room windows, an overeager search at the Texas border, a persistent antibiotic-resistant dose of the clap that spread through the crew after a gig in New Mexico. Dubious microwave burritos, long hauls between laundry days, too much information about the bus driver's divorce. On the road again.

And then there's another song to be written about the real reason you can't wait to get on the road again. Nobody's mad because you didn't take the garbage out, acquaintances don't just drop in unannounced, neighbors don't give you the stink-eye every time the wind shifts.

The thing about being on the road is that you're not bogged down by anything. Not even bad news. You give pleasure to other people and you keep your grief to yourself.

CHAPTER 21

IF YOU DON'T KNOW ME BY NOW HAROLD MELVIN & THE BLUE NOTES

Originally released on the album *I Miss You*
(Philadelphia International, 1972)
Written by Kenny Gamble and Leon Huff

IN THIS SONG THE PROTAGONIST has proven his worth, he's accounted for himself in all good ways, with class and distinction. He's performed wonders for his steady mate, gave her a life, made her rich, fed and clothed her, contributed to her happiness, but even after all this, she still doesn't trust him, thinks he's on an ego trip. She's got a short fuse and she's jumpy, every little thing leads to a blowup, there's no meeting of the minds.

This song has got a lot of bluster, a lot of conceit, a lot of hot air. It's beautifully arranged and performed to perfection. This is a song of self-pride, self-admiration.

You arrive home late, but you come at the eleventh hour with bells on, and you're in top form. You play around, but all the hanky-panky fizzles out. You're not conscious of each other. You try hard to get through, you put your cards on the table, faceup. You're considerate and up front about absolutely everything. You lay yourself bare, what is she so pissed about.

You lay in bed at night, feel her huge body—she's covered in emeralds.

On goes the light, and she wants precise details of where you've been, and she's giving you the business, giving you bad vibes. You try to be cool, but she's cagey and skeptical. You're here body and soul, why can't she get the hang of that. You've given her everything you can lay your hands on, and she still can't tune in to you. If she doesn't know you by now, she must be mindless.

Yes, knowing somebody can be a herculean task, a lot of obstacles get in the way. Still though you have to wonder, if she doesn't know your accomplishments and crowning achievements by now, will she ever. You have some mixed attitudes over the same exact things, and that leads to more arguments. More arguments to muddle through, she throws a fit about nothing and becomes your nemesis, she's got a blazing temper, and finds fault with everything. It's difficult to say how badly you feel about this, you amuse her, inspire, and gratify her, but she thinks that you're just too wrapped up in yourself, being narcissistic.

Both of you know the difference between what's right and what's not so right, neither of you were born yesterday. You're not babes in the woods— juvenile brats. Neither of you want this love to peter out. Come on now let's pull together, let's not take things for granted, let's be levelheaded here, let's not act like children. What are we grumbling about. One thing you know for sure is that you like this place, it's where you want to be, it's familiar to you. Your needs are fulfilled here, it's your shelter and stomping ground. But if she doesn't think that you'd walk out of here in a minute, she's thinking wrong, and that's just one more piece of evidence that she doesn't know you.

There's a lot of realism in this song, a lot of self-worship.

It's a song of misunderstanding and friction between people, a lopsided relationship, two partners annoying each other. Wasting time and energy over things they should leave alone. It's a long suffering and passive kind of song.

★ ★

ONE OF THE REASONS PEOPLE TURN away from

God is because religion is no longer in the fabric of their lives. It is presented as a thing that must be journeyed to as a chore—it's Sunday, we have to go to church. Or, it is used as a weapon of threat by political nutjobs on either side of every argument. But religion used to be in the water we drank, the air we breathed. Songs of praise were as spine-tingling as, and in truth the basis of, songs of carnality. Miracles illuminated behavior and weren't just spectacle.

It wasn't always a seamless interaction. Supposedly, early readers of the Bible were disturbed by the harshness of God's behavior against Job, but the prologue with God's wager with Satan about Job's piety in the face of continued testing, added later, makes it one of the most exciting and inspirational books of the Old or New Testament.

Context is everything. Helping people fit things into their lives is so much more effective than slamming them down their throats. Here's another way to look at a love song.

CHAPTER 22

THE LITTLE WHITE CLOUD THAT CRIED JOHNNIE RAY

Originally released as a single
(Okeh, 1951)
Written by Johnnie Ray

THE LITTLE WHITE CLOUD SHEDS TEARS, and bawls like a baby. You've heard its mournful lament, when walking down by the river, but you too had a heavy heart, so you were only half listening. You too were lonesome and dispirited.

The cloud tells you don't worry, all things will blow away, everything will eventually glide by and outdistance what's behind. The little cloud is feeling dismal—it's been isolated and deserted, estranged from other clouds, no one's interested in it, and it feels the effects of discrimination. On top of that, it's frightened of the booming noise from down below, the rumbling uproar, snarling and growling. The phosphorous blaze of a blinding light has shattered its vision, the glare from down under is burning through its soul. The little cloud wants to hide itself, lay low and hole up somewhere, and get out of the way. This white cloud is so unhappy, but you don't want to be dragged into its misery, if you sympathize too much, you could lose your senses. This cloud can make you sleepy.

Suddenly without warning it tells you to be still and look up, it's the sun alone that you must acknowledge. It's unchanging, unbroken, and enduring to the last. It tells you to be observant of the weather, with all its varieties. Try to harmonize yourself with it, adapt with it and you'll triumph in the end, and come out ahead.

Then it says it has a message for the world, that we all must yield to love. It tells you to spread this information to the far corners of the earth. You're not sure if you're up to this task. You don't want to say you won't, but you don't want to say you will either. You don't want to make promises or raise expectations. You also know that at any time this cloud could turn into a raging black fog that could cover the entire world, overshadow the whole planet, eclipse the sun, and behave like a tyrant. You'll have to think about it.

The message from this little white cloud to the world, that it must yield to love, giving an earful of that to the masses could backfire. To be sure, this dispatch from the little white cloud to the world can't be complicated, it must be plain and simple.

★ ★

A LOT OF PEOPLE THOUGHT when they heard Johnnie Ray

singing that he was a girl. Johnnie sang in his natural voice, which was anything but falsetto. A lot of people think male singers who sing in falsetto are actually females. Some of the Motown singers do have that quality. In Johnnie's case, though, he just sounded like a girl.

It was hard to beat him emotionally. He went through a lot of changes when he was performing, slamming piano lids down, breaking microphone stands, wrenching his heart out . . . a dynamic performer in anyone's book. Pre-Elvis. Unlike Tony Bennett, Frank or Dino, Johnnie wore his heart on his sleeve.

Not only does the little white cloud cry but he talks, and he wants me to tell the whole world how hard he tries.

This song is deceptive. It starts off so simple, like a lullaby that anyone thinks they can sing, but by the time he ascends into the middle part, he is in that rarefied air where only he and maybe Roy Orbison live. But there is no country in Johnnie's voice. It is the voice of a damaged angel cast out to walk the streets of the dirty cities, singing and squealing, crying and cajoling, banging mic stands and piano stools.

Johnnie Ray wore a hearing aid and it made him insecure, nervous. He was misunderstanding what was said and unsure he was making himself clear. Perhaps that is why his songs are full of such big notes—there is no mistaking the emotions, neither in the lyrics nor in the delivery. He didn't just wear his emotions on his sleeve, he carried them on a flag that he waved in the audience's face.

Amazingly, this song was the B-side of Johnnie's big hit "Cry." You would think there were enough tears on one side of the record, but no. The record came out on Okeh, which was mostly an R & B label. But Johnny transcended color—his feelings were too direct-hotwired from his brain for a mere pop record.

The tradition of lead singers breaking down in tears during a performance is a long one. Here's a list of songs where it happens. Some predate Johnnie, some come after him. Johnnie's records didn't need crocodile tears, no false emotions. Johnnie just let his hair down. And we all cried.

★ ★ ★ ★ ★ ★ ★ ★ ★ ★ ★ **THOSE WHO CRY** ★ ★ ★ ★ ★ ★ ★ ★ ★ ★ ★

"Don't Leave Me"—Tommy Brown

"Baby, Don't Turn Your Back on Me"—Lloyd Price and His Orchestra

"The Bells"—Billy Ward and His Dominoes (featuring Clyde McPhatter)

"Blue Eyes"—Fisher Hendley and His "Aristocratic Pigs"
(singing and bawling by Baby Ray)

"The Chicken Astronaut"—The Five Du-Tones

"Cryin' Emma"—Rolling Crew

"Cryin' for My Baby"—Pete McKinley

"Crying Like a Fool"—Jerry McCain

"Darling"—The Lyrics

"Death of an Angel"—Donald Woods and the Vel-Aires

"Frank, This Is It"—Cliff Jackson and Jellean Delk with the Naturals

"Get High"—La Melle Prince

"Go Ahead"—Billy Miranda

"I Wanna Know"—Nolan Strong and the Diablos

"It's Too Late"—Tarheel Slim and Little Ann

"Laughing But Crying"—Roy Brown

"Martha Mae"—Jack Davis and His Blues Blasters featuring Joe Frazier

"Much Too Late"—Tarheel Slim and Little Ann

"No One to Love Me"—Sha-Weez

"One More Kiss"—Paul Gayten

"The Quarrel"—The Newlyweds

"Shedding Tears for You"—Vernon Green and the Medallions

"Valerie"—Jackie and the Starlites

"Valerie"—The Jiving Juniors

"Weepin' and Cryin'"—The Griffin Brothers Orchestra

"Weeping Blues"—Rosco Gordon

In a way this is a song of genocide, where you're led by your nose into a nuclear war, ground zero, New Mexico where the first atom bomb was tested.

CHAPTER 23

EL PASO
MARTY ROBBINS

Originally released on the album *Gunfighter Ballads and Trail Songs*
(Columbia, 1959)
Written by Marty Robbins

THIS IS A BALLAD OF THE TORTURED SOUL, the cowboy heretic, prince of the protestants, falling in love with a smooth complexion dancing girl just like that, as fast as he can do it. The song hardly says anything you understand, but if you throw in the signs, symbols, and shapes, it hardly says anything that you don't understand.

Gunfire, blood, and sudden death, seems like a typical western ballad, is anything but. This is Moloch, the cat's eye pyramid, the underbelly of beauty, where you take away the bottom number and the others fall. The cowboy chosen one, bloody mass sacrifice, Jews of the Holocaust, Christ in the temple, the blood of Aztecs up on the altar. This song kicks you down, and before you can get up, it hits you again. This is the stuff to live for, and what you make of it all. This is mankind created in the image of a jealous godhead. This is fatherhood, the devil god, and the golden calf—the godly man, a jealous human being. This mode of life is an all-confrontational mode of life, the highs and lows of it, what it actually is. Truth that needs no proof, where every need is an evil need. This is a ballad of outrageous love.

El Paso—the passageway, the escape hatch, the secret staircase—ritual crime and symbolic lingo—circular imagery, names and numbers, transmigration, deportation, and all in the cryptic first person, the primitive self. The stench of perfume, alcohol, a puff of smoke, the duel, the worthless life, pain in the heart, staying in the saddle, love in vain, the grim reaper, and a love that's stronger than death, and other things. The black knight and the white knight, the good luck charm, and the evil eye. Five mounted cowboys, twelve more on the hill, and there's more—queen of sin street, diseased prostitute, an apparition that's solidly real. Heals emotionally disturbed people and the mentally ill, an invisible force, this is a woman you're willing to stake your life on.

Rosa's Cantina is the same cantina over and over again. The symbolic Rosa, the black gown and the bishop's ring, the bread and the wine, and the blood. The blood of Christian martyrs, blood that dyes the white rose red, racked and scourged. A Catholic song, universal, where no insult will go unchallenged. Where every trail goes cold, where Rome has spoken.

The handsome young stranger, foreigner, dixie democrat, maybe twenty years younger, with his hands all over the snake worshipping Felina, dead on the floor. Killed by the quick-drawing cowboy with ferocious intent, shot him dead not a split second too late, with a wink and a nod. A mixed bag of a man, a magpie. To not have done so would be a violation of an age-old custom, practically a sacrilege. Don't think there wasn't any good in him, Felina might say with a heartfelt sigh. You bury your face in the crotch of your elbow—it's impossible to feel overjoyed. You hustle out the back door and steal a fine horse—fleeing in haste, northward and into the Badlands, into the chaos and climax of the song, you're going as fast as you can, but it's not all that fast.

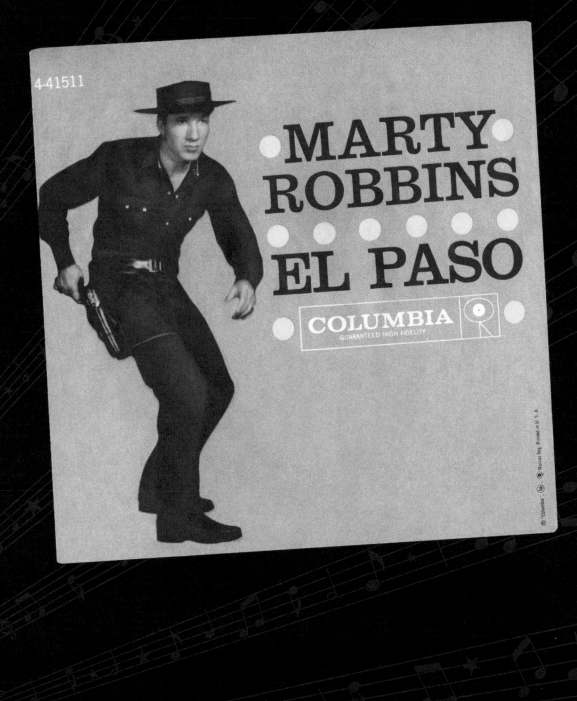

In a way this is a song of genocide, where you're led by your nose into a nuclear war, ground zero, New Mexico where the first atom bomb was tested. Land of witchcraft, Crazy Cat Mountain, and the El Paso gate of death. Tierra del Encanto, near the white sand missile range, the devils' highway, down Jornada del Muerto. It's a labyrinth of a song, it's the end of the line for Roy Rogers, king of the cowboys. The end of beans, bacon and meat, bedrolls, and cow roping—code of the west and the longhorn drive. The end of the sheik, the gaucho, and the matador—where one bad bull will be the death of you, the lonely figure, and the scamp—the cowboy scapegoat and this is his story.

At last you're free forevermore, and far away out of it all. The smoke's cleared and you're a lot better than you thought you'd be, but you can't help notice something's missing. The black eyed Felina is still in your mind, and she's calling out in a whisper, I want you over here right away. So you saddle up and away you go—it's your duty. Back over the shifting sands, into the high speed whirlwind romance that you left behind, until you're looking down on Rosa's Cantina from up on the bluff, but then from out of the blue, five mounted cowboys are shooting at you. They're larger than life. Vigilantes with badges pursuing you. Not for slaying and killing, not for the taking of life, not for the routine charge of murder, but for horse stealing, the old west capital crime. They pump you full of lead and shoot you off your horse. It's there that Felina finds you, and takes her place beside you, kissing your cheek while you're slowly dying—cradles you in her two loving arms, lays her hands on you and kisses your lips, and you kiss her back, with a kiss that says I forgive you.

This is a post resurrection song, and it flies above your head.

MARTY ROBBINS STEPPED ONTO THE SCENE

in the 1950s with "A White Sport Coat and a Pink Carnation." An undeniable, infectious, melodic hit song that would appeal to everybody. He'd tried to get into the rockabilly scene before that, making some competent records, like "Maybelline," "That's All Right, Mama" and "Singing the Blues." But that was just Marty starting out. "White Sport Coat" is a mystical song. The color white and the color pink both have symbolic meaning.

Marty Robbins had an ace up his sleeve. His grandfather Robert "Texas" Heckle, commonly known as Texas Bob, was an actual Confederate soldier in the Civil War, serving in the First Texas Infantry Regiment. After the war, Texas Bob served under Generals Custer and Crook in the Indian territories of Montana and Wyoming.

He was an illustrious frontier poet, a rough-hewn man who wrote of the great expansion as one who had lived it and whose books told the stories of the men and women who extended the boundaries of the United States. As can be seen from the cover of one of his books, *Rhymes of the Frontier*, Texas Bob was the archetypal medicine-show cowboy—tall and lean in the saddle, shoulder-length silver hair under a Confederate soldier's hat, skin weathered by wind and sun to the color and texture of his buckskin pants. He was handsome and charismatic as he spun tales for his grandson Marty—tales that he heard around the campfire, tales that others were getting only from the TV. Tales that Marty took with a grain of salt.

Marty was skeptical of his grandfather's tall tales—he credited Texas Bob with being a better yarn spinner than truth teller. But that didn't make him love or listen any less. And Texas Bob's stories of buckshot and bludgeons in the border towns of Texas held the young boy's attention the way Roy Rogers's big-screen adventures were holding his classmates'. Beer and blood splashed across the adobe walls of the cantinas in the tales Texas Bob told, and Marty learned young that the truth had little to do with a good story. Or a good song.

"My grandfather wrote stories, but he couldn't write melodies, so I started off writing melodies to the stories he told me."

Eventually when the field cleared, and the opportunity arose, Marty delivered this, a song called "El Paso" that resonates on every level with people on every level. People talk about message songs, starting with Woody Guthrie and right up through the sixties. But "El Paso" is the ultimate message song, and reflective words would only hope to scratch the surface. It is so complex, yet it is so simple in its construction—this is a dark tale of indescribable beauty and death.

"El Paso" is built on five stanzas, each one two verses and a bridge and then returning to the next stanza. What makes it unusual are the pickup phrases between the end of the bridge and the next verse, short preludes that propel you into the ongoing story. These phrases are as important as any other words in the song. You can accept this song as the lovely lament of a dying cowboy, drifting through exotic places and dying for a dancing girl that he hardly knows, or not.

Sound the alarm for the salt of the earth and play the anthems for the glory and majesty that has gone the way of all flesh.

CHAPTER 24

NELLY WAS A LADY
ALVIN YOUNGBLOOD HART

Originally released on the compilation
Beautiful Dreamer: The Songs of Stephen Foster
(American Roots Publishing/Emergent Music Marketing, 2004)
Written by Stephen Foster

IN THIS SONG THE FIRE'S GONE OUT and your life is missing. Your happiness has turned to nothing—there's no trace of it. Your happiness is out and out over.

You're hauling the timber on the grand river, the big river, river of tears, manifest destiny—you hoist the cottonwood logs, the silver bark poplars, that make bright shiny tables and furniture, but you've reached the station in life where the work is meaningless, and it's been this way ever since grief came to knock. Knocking when the cock crowed—grief and gloom in the first light of morning, knocking out the bright lights of the heavens.

Now you live life absent minded and distracted, but you won't give in to emotions, if you did you'd be sunk. You're never going to be sunk or go under, you're never going to lose balance, even in this, the collapse of your world. Now and forever, you'll be lukewarm to all things in life—in the face of this heavy blow.

Let's strike the bell for stateliness and virtue and let the sirens ring for what's proper and priceless. Sound the alarm for the salt of the earth and play the anthems for the glory and majesty that has gone the way of all flesh. The beaming smiling face that expired once and for all, your better half, your genuine counterpart. In your mind you're meandering through the meadows, the green pastures—the hanging branches among the clover, the blooming bouquets of a summer day, and right along side you is everything you love, everything fine and fair—all that is true and trustworthy, everything natural.

You're roaming the fields and listening to the funeral hymns. You never lose sight of her face, your precious treasure, your reason for being, taken away that day in the black wagon. Your excitement for life has faded away, but still above all, there's the daily grind. You never put any more effort out into anything, except what's necessary. All life's colors have darkened, and your bones feel like they're on the body of a ghost.

★ ★

STEPHEN FOSTER IS THE COUNTERPART TO

Edgar Allan Poe. This is one sweeping song that is designed to make anybody who's ever lived a life just lie down and weep. A lot of sad songs have been written but none sadder than this. Both the lyrics and the melody. Alvin Youngblood Hart's is as good a version as you'll ever hear. Alvin sings the song in its pure form.

The guitar turnarounds are a slow cakewalk between heartbroken verses, loss shared on the front porch. The tune will stay in your head long after you have forgotten the story and every time you hum it a tear will roll down your cheek.

CHAPTER 25

CHEAPER TO KEEP HER
JOHNNIE TAYLOR

Originally released on the album *Taylored in Silk*

(Stax, 1973)

Written by Mack Rice

SOUL RECORDS, LIKE HILLBILLY, BLUES, calypso, Cajun, polka, salsa, and other indigenous forms of music, contain wisdom that the upper crust often gets in academia. The so-called school of the streets is a real thing and it doesn't just apply to learning to steer clear of hustlers and charlatans. While Ivy League graduates talk about love in a rush of quatrains detailing abstract qualities and gossamer attributes, folks from Trinidad to Atlanta, Georgia, sing of the benefits of making an ugly woman your wife and the cold hard facts of life.

Or, in this case, Johnnie Taylor saves you a hefty legal consultation fee by telling you that it's cheaper to keep her.

Of course it's cheaper to keep her. How could it not be? Divorce is a ten-billion-dollar-a-year industry. And that's without renting a hall, hiring a band or throwing bouquets. Even without the cake that's a lot of dough.

If you're lucky enough to get into this racket, you can make a fortune manipulating the laws and helping destroy relationships between people who at one point or another swore undying love to one another. Nobody knows how to pull the plug on this golden goose, nor do they really want to. Most especially not those who risk nothing but who keep raking it in.

Marriage and divorce are currently played out in the courtrooms and on the tongues of gossips; the very nature of the institution has become warped and distorted, a gotcha game of vitriol and betrayal.

How many divorce lawyers are parties to this betrayal between two supposedly civilized people? The honest answer is all of them. This would be an unimportant economic slugfest if it was just between the estranged parties. After all, marriage is a pretty simple contract—till death do you part. Right there is the reason that God-fearing members of the community regularly gave divorced folks the skunk-eye. If they were willing to disavow that basic a contract, what makes you think they won't disavow anything and everything? That's why historically, if you were a divorced person nobody trusted you.

Marriage is the only contract that can be dissolved because interest fades or because someone purposefully behaves badly. If you're an engineer for Google, for example, you can't just wander over to another company and start working there because it's suddenly more attractive. There's promises and responsibilities and the new company would have to buy out your contract. But people seldom think logically when breaking up a home.

Married or not, however, a parent has a duty to support a child. And this matters a whole lot more than divvying up summer homes. Ultimately, marriage is for the sake of those children. And a couple who has no children, that's not a family. They are just two friends; friends with benefits and insurance coverage but just friends nonetheless.

But divorce lawyers don't care about familial bonds; they are, by definition, in the destruction business. They destroy families. How many of them are at least tangentially responsible for teen suicides and serial killers? Like generals who don't have to see the boys they send to war, they feign innocence with blood on their hands.

They say married by the Bible, divorced by the law—but will your lawyer talk to God for you? The laws of God override the laws of man every time but clearing the moneylenders from the temple is one thing—getting them out of your life is another. If people could get away from the legal costs, they might have a better chance to keep their heads above water.

And then there are prenuptial agreements. You might as well play black-jack against a crooked casino. Two people at the height of their ardor lay a bet that those feelings won't last. They pay lawyers to make sure that whoever has the most assets has that money protected when they start getting mad at each other. Now, those same lawyers will tell you that it's just a precaution and in many cases these agreements never have to get implemented. But look a little closer and what you realize is these lawyers have even figured out how to get paid way in advance, and indeed, in lieu, of a divorce.

So, is there a solution? Perhaps.

Mixed marriages, gay marriages—proponents have rightly lobbied to make all of these legal but no one has fought for the only one that really counts, the polygamist marriage.

It's nobody's business how many wives a man has. Muslims can have four wives. South Africans can have as many as ten. Brigham Young had fifty children by who knows how many wives. No telling how many children the Sheik of Araby spawned. Screamin' Jay Hawkins left behind something like seventy-five with almost as many women. In the biblical sense a man can have as many wives as he can afford. If he's poverty stricken, he's not going to have too many wives, if any. But if he's King Solomon he can have three hundred wives. It all depends on who you are and who you know. Divorce is the key issue if anyone cares to know.

A man pays alimony to one bride and then he has to support another. He goes from that wife to another and now he's paying alimony times two and supporting a third. Now, he has a flock of wives to support.

Of course, this would be true with or without lawyers. It's just common sense. But it doesn't end there. The lawyers just add to the confusion and the expense. But the screws already get tightened from all sides—women's rights crusaders and women's lib lobbyists take turns putting man back on his heels until he is pinned behind the eight ball dodging the shrapnel from the smashed glass ceiling.

You can almost hear the gnashing of teeth and snarls from the crusaders and lobbyists. But before the feminists chase me through the village with torches, consider these two points.

First, what downtrodden woman with no future, battered around by the whims of a cruel society, wouldn't be better off as one of a rich man's wives—taken care of properly, rather than friendless on the street depending on government stamps?

And second, when did I ever posit that the polygamist marriage had to be male singular female plural? Have at it, ladies. There's another glass ceiling for you to break.

It's cheaper to keep her indeed.

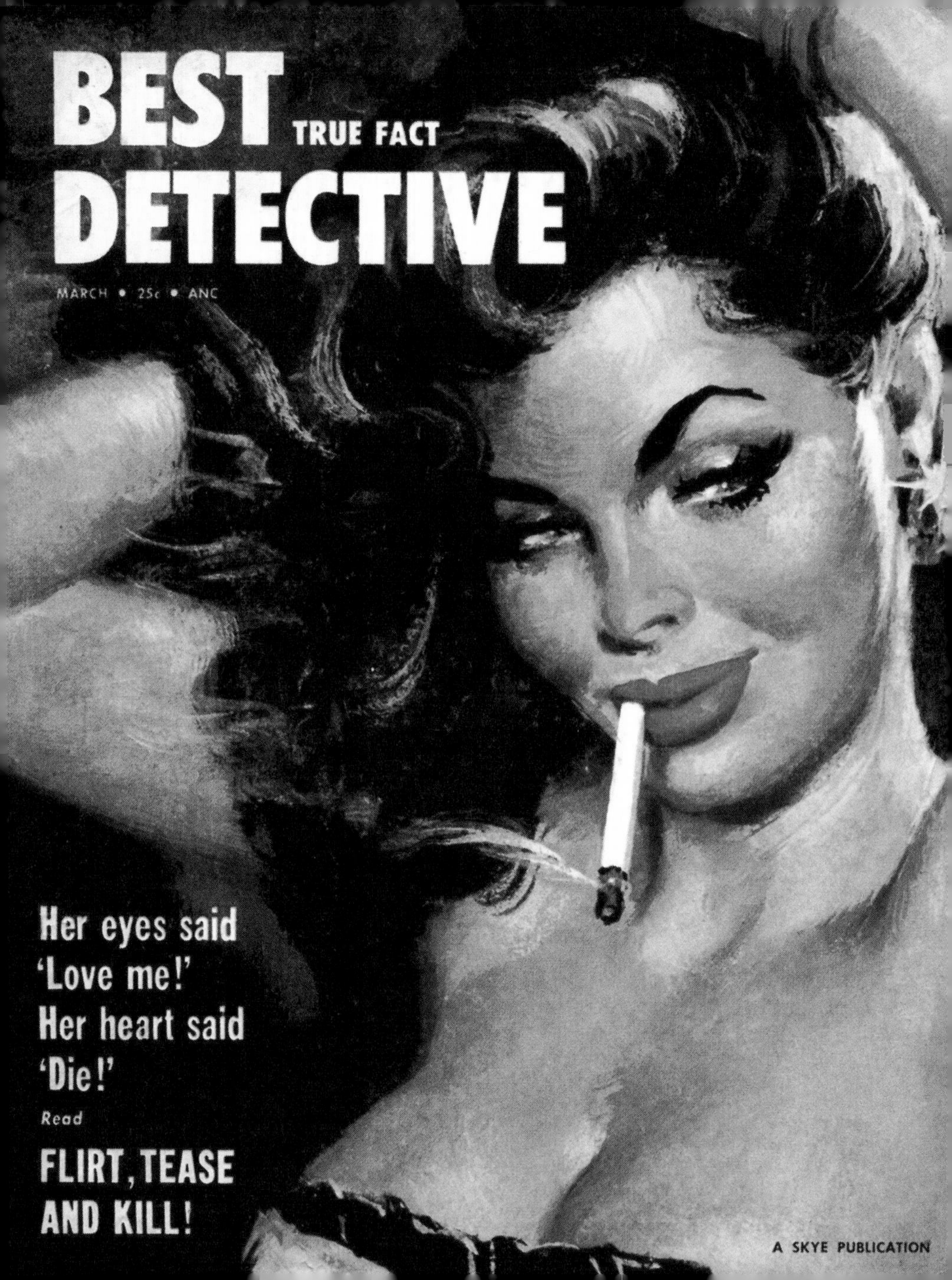

BEST TRUE FACT

DETECTIVE

MARCH • 25¢ • ANC

Her eyes said
'Love me!'
Her heart said
'Die!'

Read

FLIRT, TEASE
AND KILL!

A SKYE PUBLICATION

CHAPTER 26

I GOT A WOMAN RAY CHARLES

Originally released as a single
(Atlantic, 1954)
Written by Ray Charles and Renald Richard

HALF A BLOCK FROM THE INTERSECTION and
the yellow light was already stale. Didn't really matter, traffic was already stop-
and-go even without the traffic signals' being against him. Was gonna take
three hours at this rate. Probably could've stopped and had dinner after leaving work and gotten there at the same time. But she was waiting for him.

Late afternoon sun hotter than a match head but the ride was long enough
for the sweat-soaked shirt sticking to his car seat to dry out. He patted his
pocket to make sure he had a stick of gum to pop into his mouth as he turned
down her street. But that was still a long way off. He turned up the radio and
tapped the steering wheel in time to Fathead Newman's tenor saxophone.

His head hurt from too much coffee. He thought about the new girl at
work, the one with the high cheekbones and the Band-Aid on her heel where
her shoe rubbed her raw. She smiled when she held the elevator for him. She
probably lived nearby. Why couldn't he like her?

In the beginning he drove recklessly, desire rolling him through stop signs before he settled into the torpor of habit and the drive became a chore and not a mission.

She would be waiting for him, half asleep and cranky on the couch. It's not like he was gonna be great company either after driving way over town. Sure, in the early days it was peaches. Love day and night, never grumblin' or fussin'. But that wears off quick. And then the only thing left is the long drive.

Desire fades but traffic goes on forever.

CHAPTER 27

CIA MAN
THE FUGS

Originally released on the album *Virgin Fugs*
(ESP-Disk, 1967)
Written by Tuli Kupferberg

———————

SAM PHILLIPS WOULD'VE LOVED THIS record.

He couldn't have released it but would have wished he'd recorded it—maybe with Jerry Lee, who wouldn't have known what to make of it either, but would've been glad to have recorded it and boogied it up like nobody's business. It definitely would have been an underground hit. The lyrics are anything but generic ("Who can kill a general in his bed . . . Overthrow dictators if they're Red . . . Fuckin'-A man . . . CIA man"). If these lyrics don't get your attention, then you must be comatose. It's amazing how powerful the Fugs could be with just a few edgy instruments.

This song turns a CIA man into a comic book character. You kind of have to wonder why DC Comics or Marvel didn't come up with a CIA man. Stan Lee would have had a ball drawing up this guy. This record is the paranoiac's flip side to Johnny Rivers's "Secret Agent Man." But this is much stronger and more to the point.

Buying records by the Fugs was like buying some Sun Ra records; you had no idea what you would get. One record would sound pretty slick—well, as slick as they could sound—but slick as in recorded in a studio with a band that stopped and started at the same time. Then you'd pick up another release and it sounded like it was recorded by a tomato can telephone on the end of a broom handle. Seems like the Fugs could record anywhere, and sometimes the liner notes on their albums were in Esperanto. They dared you to figure out what they were about.

One of the ways creativity works is the brain tries to fill in holes and gaps. We fill in missing bits of pictures, snatches of dialogue, we finish rhymes and invent stories to explain things we do not know. When you don't know who Johnny Pissoff or a Slum Goddess is, when you have no clue about Coca-Cola douches, your imagination just fires away.

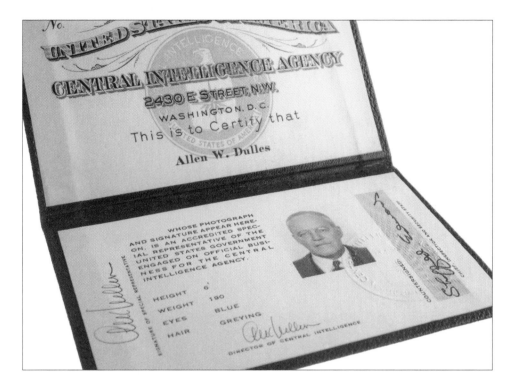

The Fugs recorded this song a couple of times—live and slick and weird and primitive. They're both good and right on the money.

The Fugs get their name from a Norman Mailer novel called *The Naked and the Dead*. When *The Naked and the Dead* came out in 1948, censorship rules at the time forced Mailer to substitute the word fug for fuck. The Fugs could have just as well called themselves the Fucks but decided to go the safer route so the records could be purchased in a record store and not in a back alley.

Norman Mailer or the Fugs notwithstanding, the word fug never caught on as a substitute for fuck. You don't say fug you or what the fug or that ain't no fuggin' good. We still use the proper terminology.

You get the feeling the Fugs never used all their real talent or strength at any one time. You always felt they were holding something back and could explode at any moment.

How long will it take before you realize that your idle life is one of indulgence, but then again, what do you have to lose?

CHAPTER 28

ON THE STREET WHERE YOU LIVE VIC DAMONE

Originally released as a single
(Columbia, 1956)
Music by Frederick Loewe
Lyrics by Alan Jay Lerner

YOU GOT A HABIT, A BAD HABIT. You fell in love with the hard stuff. You fell for the foxy harlot, the vamp who lives around here somewhere, and you're silly about her, she's got you hooked.

You're on the street where she lives, the back alley. You don't know exactly where she lives, but it's around here somewhere. You've roamed every passageway, examining the street from A to Z, just like in the days of old, you're walking on the same old ground, nothing changed. But suddenly everything does. The pavement which has always been beneath your feet flies up out of nowhere, and it's wrong side up. You're blasted sky high into a tall building, a real cloud buster. When you look down below everything looks tiny and insignificant, even the street where she lives, you see yourself on it, a nonentity a nonbeing. Then you get slammed back down into reality, you take the long fall, hitting the cement like an express train, but you don't have a scratch on you, so everything must still be in order. Then you pick up where you left off. Walking down dark alleys, looking into lobbies and hallways, in the hope to get a glimpse of her, and you've often walked down that street before.

Is this really the street where she lives? It has to be her street because the birds are singing here, and there couldn't be birds singing on any other street. You still have some sense of direction, so you start to walk again. Are there lilac trees in this part of town—you think about it, but the thought is short-lived. People stop and stare but that doesn't bother you, you're on a head trip and you're too spaced out to notice. They gawk at you, and gossip, give you the evil eye. But it doesn't reach any deep part of you. You're not going to go out of your way to acknowledge any of it. The scrutiny doesn't even remotely touch you. There's no place on the planet you'd rather be, than on this dead-end street, the street where she lives.

How long will it take before you realize that your idle life is one of indulgence, but then again, what do you have to lose? The longer you don't see her, the less chance you have to offend her, that's the way you look at it. Let the clock keep ticking, what do you care. All in a split second, everything could change again. You're on the street where she lives. You could be on any street in the world, but you're partial to this one. It's an ancient street, it's antiquated, and it's been around, and you have to stay on good terms with it. You have to make it your friend.

★ ★

THIS SONG IS ALL ABOUT the three-syllable rhyme: street before, feet before, heart of town, part of town, bother me, rather be. You can make up your own: here at last, clear at last, ring that bell, what's that smell? Make it rhyme, any old time. Vic Damone. Sick at home.

Maybe that's as close as you can get with somebody. Being on the street where they live. Maybe you're thinking that anytime that person could appear, you are that close. Maybe you just wait all night and all day too. Maybe a cop car would come by and ask you what you're doing there. If you tell him the truth, that you're just waiting to see somebody, you'll probably be arrested for stalking. Depends on who it is. You could be stalking somebody in the South Bronx—being on the street where they live. How long you are going to be waiting there is anybody's guess.

If you could sing like Vic Damone, maybe you could buy your way out. Vic Damone married Pier Angeli way back in the fifties. Pier Angeli was the love of James Dean's life. Legend says that he waited across the street on his motorcycle on Pier Angeli's wedding day. That says something about life—when Pier Angeli could go from somebody like James Dean to Vic Damone in the blink of an eye. You have to wonder what the connection was. Did she see something of Jimmy in Vic Damone? Or, did she just need to get as far away as possible?

Maybe for the rest of his short life, this was a song that belonged to James Dean.

CHAPTER 29

TRUCKIN'
THE GRATEFUL DEAD

Originally released as a single and on the album *American Beauty*
(Warner Bros., 1970)
Music by Jerry Garcia, Bob Weir, and Phil Lesh
Lyrics by Robert Hunter

THE GRATEFUL DEAD ARE NOT YOUR USUAL

rock and roll band. They're essentially a dance band. They have more in common with Artie Shaw and bebop than they do with the Byrds or the Stones. Whirling dervish dancers are as much a part of their music as anything else. There is a big difference in the types of women that you see from the stage when you are with the Stones compared to the Dead. With the Stones it's like being at a porno convention. With the Dead, it's more like the women you see by the river in the movie *O Brother, Where Art Thou?* Free floating, snaky and slithering like in a typical daydream. Thousands of them. With most bands the audience participates like in a spectator sport. They just stand there and watch. They keep a distance. With the Dead, the audience is part of the band— they might as well be on the stage.

The Dead are from a different world than their contemporaries. Jefferson Airplane, Quicksilver Messenger Service, Big Brother, all of them together wouldn't even make a part of the Dead. What makes them essentially a dance band probably begins with the jazz classical bassist, Phil Lesh, and the Elvin Jones–influenced Bill Kreutzmann. Lesh is one of the most skilled bassists you'll ever hear in subtlety and invention. And combined with Kreutzmann, this rhythm section is hard to beat. That rhythm section along with elements of traditional rock and roll and American folk music is what makes the Dead unsurpassable. Combined with their audience, it's like one big free-floating ballet. Three main singers, two drummers and triple harmonies make this band difficult to compete with. A postmodern jazz musical rock and roll dynamo.

Then there's Bob Weir. A very unorthodox rhythm player. Has his own style, not unlike Joni Mitchell but from a different place. Plays strange, augmented chords and half chords at unpredictable intervals that somehow match up with Jerry Garcia—who plays like Charlie Christian and Doc Watson at the same time. All that and an in-house writer-poet, Robert Hunter, with a wide range of influences—everyone from Kerouac to Rilke—and steeped in the songs of Stephen Foster. This creates a wide range of opportunities for the Dead to play almost any kind of music and make it their own.

"Truckin'" is one of their signature songs and lyrically it combines the goings-on of a wild and wide world. The Doo Dah man even appears in this song. "I came down south with my hat caved in." This could easily be a Dead song from one hundred years earlier.

When you go to a Dead concert you are right there in Pirate Alley on the Barbary Coast, right there by the San Francisco Bay. At any time you could drop through a trapdoor into a rowboat and be shanghaied to China and not even know it. This song, even though it lists some cities, has very little to do with Chuck Berry's "Promised Land," Martha and the Vandellas' "Dancing in the Street," or even Hank Snow's "I've Been Everywhere." This song is all on the same street. Chicago, New York, Detroit, New Orleans, Houston, Buffalo. It's all the same main street. Long before America had actually transformed itself into the same sprawling mall.

This song is medium tempo, but it seems to just keep picking up speed. It's got a fantastic first verse, which doesn't let up or fizzle out, and every verse that follows could actually be a first verse. Arrows of neon, flashing marquees, Dallas and a soft machine, Sweet Jane, vitamin C, Bourbon Street, bowling pins, hotel windows, and the classic line, "What a long strange trip it's been." A thought that anybody can relate to. Cards that ain't worth a dime. All in the same town. But you're moving anyway. The lyrics just pile up on top of each other. But the meaning is understandable and clear. The song also changes pace and changes back and the chorus has got that triple harmony again. "Truckin'"—it conjures up something different from traveling. It's arduous. But the Dead are a swinging dance band so it doesn't seem like hard work to go with them.

The guy singing the song acts and talks like who he is, and not the way others would want him to talk and act.

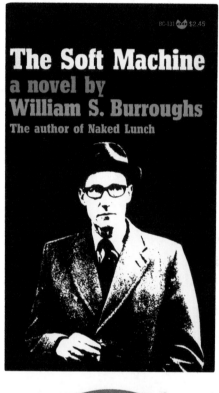

All things considered you're hitched up for good, she's your dream girl—you're her best man and you're hanging on to her for dear life.

CHAPTER 30

RUBY, ARE YOU MAD? OSBORNE BROTHERS

Originally released as a single

(MGM, 1956)

Written by Cousin Emmy (Cynthia May Carver)

THIS SONG SPEAKS IN THE MOTHER TONGUE,

at breakneck speed—rapid quick fire, hardcore, and irresistible—close as it comes to alchemy and reckons what it's worth. Right on point, it's keen to drive you mad, and it's all about Ruby.

Ruby, the gal who can restore to you whatever you've lost and then make you lose it again. Ruby is just as she is, switched on, plugged in and lady like.

You're sitting in the shade, slumped out, anonymous, incognito, watching everything go by, unimpressed, hard-bitten—impenetrable. You can see what people ought to do, but they're not the things that you ought to do, the difference between you and them is like the difference between night and day. You're marching in different parades. This song is church Latin, has plenty of backbone, and pieces of the whirlwind in it.

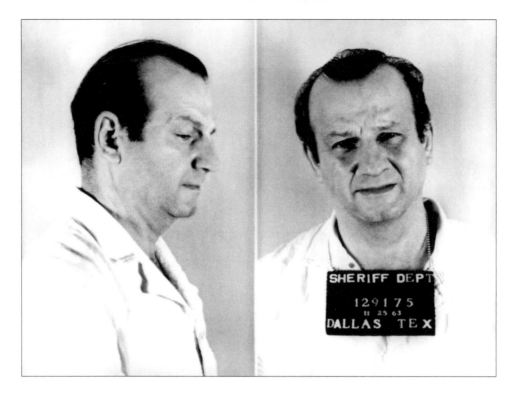

You're the rakish king of life and Ruby is the royal queen. She is jam packed, full bodied, mellow, top-heavy and in her prime, and you're in on the ground floor. She's quick witted and has bailed you out of many a tight situation. No statue could be as beautiful, and any description would be an understatement. She's not mad at anybody, calls you snookums, and you call her buttercup, she spoofs you, pulls your leg, she's your baby doll.

This song is well composed, relentless, and slick. Don't be conned by the shovel and spade. This song comes down the pike at lightning speed, jet fueled, played by wizards at full throttle with blazing motivation.

You might have had a squabble with Ruby once, but that's ancient history.

All things considered you're hitched up for good, she's your dream girl—you're her best man and you're hanging on to her for dear life. This song excavates deep down into the old guard establishment, with the shovel and spade, cracking up and grinning all the way. The song does not depend on one single thing to get by, it has a jillion things to get by, and it doubles down on it all.

★ ★

RUBY, ARE YOU MAD AT YOUR MAN? Ruby, don't

take your love to town. "Ruby My Dear," "Ruby Tuesday," "Ruby Baby." What is it about the name Ruby? It's not even a real name. A rube is someone that's an easy mark. Easy to take for a ride. Someone who'll buy anything. You appeal to their emotions and fantasies, and you can sell them anything. And then there's Jack Ruby. Ruby, are you mad at your man—you could translate the song any kinda way. Ruby, are you mad at your man—well I guess so. What'd you do that for?

The Osborne Brothers are a high-powered bluegrass group. Maybe the most high. Roy Orbison couldn't hold a note as long as this guy who is singing high tenor. The Osborne Brothers sing extremely exquisite harmony lines. In this song, it's tough to do. There's only one chord to it, but there's plenty going on. No drums either. That just tells you that it's all rhythm. The drums will get in the way and slow you down. Orchestrated by twin fiddles, fast and tense. A song to drive your car over a cliff to, with the radio still on, and you won't feel a thing. This sounds like churchgoing harmony. Mandolin even going at full speed. You can't drive any faster than this. No melody, one key, everybody going one hundred miles an hour. Sittin' in the shade and shovelin' with a spade. Ruby, are you mad at your man? Anybody can understand this. Anybody who is anybody. And you can feel it so hard that understanding isn't necessary.

Bluegrass is the other side of heavy metal. Both are musical forms steeped in tradition. They are the two forms of music that visually and audibly have not changed in decades. People in their respective fields still dress like Bill Monroe and Ronnie James Dio. Both forms have a traditional instrumental lineup and a parochial adherence to form.

Bluegrass is the more direct emotional music and, though it might not be obvious to the casual listener, the more adventurous. On this track, Bobby Osborne's daredevil vocal swoops, sustained notes, and the drive of the twin banjos with lightning runs combined to make something so staggeringly propulsive it would most likely make Yngwie Malmsteen scratch his head. This is speed metal without the embarrassment of Spandex and junior high school devil worship.

But people confuse tradition with calcification. We listen to an old record and imagine it sealed in amber, a piece of nostalgia that exists for our own needs, without a thought of the sweat and toil, anger and blood that went into making it or the thing it may have turned into. The recording is actually merely a snapshot of those musicians at that moment. A snapshot can be riveting and artful, but it is the choice of the single moment plucked from the stream of moments that makes it immortal.

There is a recording of the Osborne Brothers at a bluegrass festival maybe ten years after this record had come out. At that point, it was just one of their hits, not the first release of their first solo record deal. The record had been good to them and they had probably played it upward of a thousand times live. They could have just gone through the motions and delivered a credible copy of the record.

Instead, the song morphed and grew. Drums were now part of the lineup and they found a way to incorporate them without gumming up the momentum. A throwaway lick played on the banjo one night was repeated and honed until it became a central riff underneath another part. It was still the same song but the tiny grace notes and elasticity kept it alive, shook the dust from its boots.

Of course, some people cried foul and those people should've stayed home. And live, as on the record, when the band stops on a dime for those wondrous, stacked harmonies before driving home with banjo fury, it is simultaneously tightly arranged and loose with giddy enthusiasm.

DL 75079

STEREO

Favorite Hymns

INCLUDING: **HOW GREAT THOU ART** · **ROCK OF AGES** · **STEAL AWAY AND PRAY**
LIGHT AT THE RIVER · **WHAT A FRIEND WE HAVE IN JESUS** · **JESUS SURE CHANGED ME**

THE OSBORNE BROTHERS

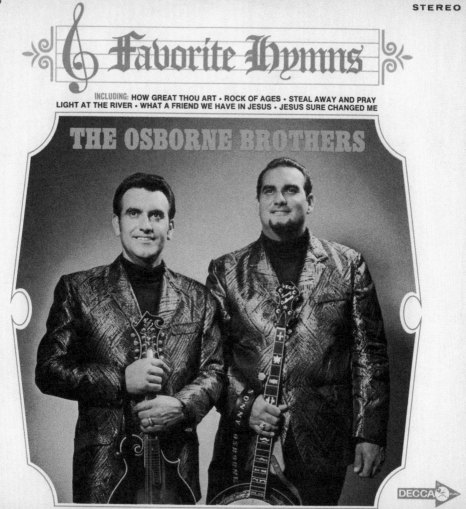

DECCA

CHAPTER 31

OLD VIOLIN
JOHNNY PAYCHECK

Originally released as a single
(Mercury, 1986)
Written by Johnny Paycheck

THERE'S LOTS OF REASONS FOLKS CHANGE

their names. Some have new names thrust upon them as part of religious ceremonies, coming-of-age rituals or arrival into new lands where the unusual diphthongs or combinations of consonants coupled with hitherto unseen umlauts and tildes force ethnic names to be shortened into blander alternatives.

And then there are those who change their own names, either on the run from some unseen demon or heading toward something else. Donald Eugene Lytle knew he was born for more than his birth name had in store. And by the time he was a teenager, his hometown of Greenfield, Ohio, could barely contain him. He had already run the table of all the local talent contests starting when he was nine years old after teaching himself how to play just about any stringed instrument.

By the mid-fifties he was playing bass and steel guitar and singing tenor harmony with big names like Ray Price and Faron Young and up-and-comers like Willie Nelson. In 1960 he had two big breakthroughs. Three, if you count changing his name to Donny Young.

Under that name, he hit the country charts, reaching number 35 with a song called "Miracle of Love." The flip side, "Shakin' the Blues," was written by the man who would give him his other big break of the year by hiring him for his band—country legend George Jones.

Both George Jones and Donny Young went through a transformation while they played together. Both of them were hopped-up hillbilly singers in the style preferred by country music producer Pappy Daily, favoring Roger Miller–style songs like "Tall Tall Trees" and "You Gotta Be My Baby."

George was a hell-raiser, prone to drink and miss a gig, but Donny was something else. He was a little guy, barely five feet and change. Like a lot of small men, he was wrapped tighter than the inside of a golf ball and hit just about as often. There was a dark cloud and a long rap sheet following Donny Young and that name was sounding too sunshiny for a man who was waking up in alleyways with tattered clothes after a three-day drunk.

In 1964, Donny took one letter and added it to the name of a Polish boxer from Chicago who faced Joe Louis for the heavyweight title in 1940 at Madison Square Garden. Johnny Paychek lost that night, but Donny Young still carried his name forward. And as in any true metamorphosis, anyone looking at the butterfly would be hard-pressed to imagine the caterpillar from whence it sprang.

Johnny Paycheck was the outlaw all the other country singers claimed to be. Perhaps it was because George Jones and Waylon Jennings were born with their names while Johnny seemed to know from birth that he was on the run and his one hope to dodge the hellhounds on his trail even for a moment was by signing in under a different name.

There was chaos and turmoil and narrow escapes but through it all there was singing that could not be denied. Many people believe that the sound that made George Jones the King of Country Music came about because George listened so closely to his ex–bass player and was more dependable. And when a guy who rides his lawn mower to the liquor store because his wife hid the car keys is more dependable, you have a sense of what country music was like at the time.

Donny Young had ditched the light breeziness of his early recordings and went into the studio with Billy Sherrill, the Nashville producer who announced he wasn't going to take your shit by slapping his .45 pistol on the eight-track board to set the boundaries.

Johnny wrote hits like Tammy Wynette's "Apartment #9," as well as classics such as "(Pardon Me) I've Got Someone to Kill," which he wrote with Aubrey Mayhew and recorded himself. Writing, recording, touring, raising hell—Johnny Paycheck was Donny Young no more.

He reached the top of the charts and became a blue-collar hero singing David Allan Coe's everyman anthem "Take This Job and Shove It."

And when the fall came, the banner headlines told of liquor, cocaine, a .22-caliber bullet that creased a man's skull, and ultimately twenty-two months in prison.

When George Strait covered "Old Violin" he said that Johnny Paycheck had written it while waiting for news about his pardon from Ohio governor Richard Celeste. It's easy to look at the lyric and imagine Johnny, in his cell, feeling like that old fiddle being set aside, never to be heard again. But songs

have a way of getting out. People like George Strait bring them to new audiences. And even better in this case, Johnny also got out. He received his pardon, went back into the studio and recorded "Old Violin." It was the most successful, but not the last, of his post-prison singles, getting all the way up to number 21.

George Strait sang it good. But he'll be the first to tell you, he didn't live it like Johnny Paycheck did. And George Jones knew enough not to even try to sing it. Some songs will fight you as hard as a person can.

Songs like this can be covered but never really owned by anyone else. If you hear someone else sing it, you might not even stop to listen, but just two lines from Paycheck freezes you in your tracks.

There's a live version from some country reunion show. Johnny is seated and his girth forces him to hold the guitar in an unusual fashion, beneath his knees. He doesn't make eye contact with any of the people around him, instead staring off into the middle distance as he sings with a voice as burnished as the wood in . . . well, an old violin.

No other country singer—Hank, Lefty, Kitty—no one could come close to this performance. He dips down to a low baritone and then goes up into that high tenor that somehow all the years of abuse didn't damage. He insinuates, leans in close to the microphone for a moment of heartfelt recitation, and at one point stops strumming so he can point to the heavens like Babe Ruth signaling Johnny Sylvester's home run, before he hits a high note as pure and as clean as a mountain stream.

People say that Sinatra was a thug who transformed into a poet when he sang. Frank sang mostly of love and loss. The stakes are higher in this song—it's about life and death.

Sometimes when songwriters write from their own lives, the results can be so specific, other people can't connect to them. Putting melodies to diaries doesn't guarantee a heartfelt song. On the other hand, Sinatra has shown us time and again, a so-called moon/June song can break your heart over and over.

"Old Violin" is different. The extended metaphor of obsolescence, of the final go-round, is so vivid, yet so simple, the words so inseparable from Johnny's performance, that knowing the story does not diminish the song at all. We all feel the pathos of the story.

This is not always the case. Polio victim Doc Pomus was in a wheelchair at his wedding, watching his bride dance with his brother, while he wrote the lyrics to "Save the Last Dance for Me." As amazing and heartbreaking as this story is, one can argue that it diminishes it as a song because it takes what used to be a universal message of love and replaces it with a very specific set of images. It's hard to have your own romance supersede Doc's once you know the poignant backstory.

This may also be the reason so few songs that were made during the video age went on to become standards; we are locked into someone else's messaging of the lyrics. But miraculously, "Old Violin" transcends.

People thought of Johnny Paycheck as a lost cause. But time and again he proved them wrong; he was just like that old violin, a Stradivarius no less, maybe the one that Paganini played. This is as gallant, generous, and faithful a performance as you'll ever hear.

IF YOU LIKE THE PLYMOUTH VALIANT...YOU'LL L♥VE THE

PLYMOUTH VOLARÉ!

Here's a book of facts — some of them surprising — about the popular Volaré, the small car with the accent on comfort. It has been prepared for people who appreciate all the good things about the Plymouth Valiant.

1973 PLYMOUTH VALIANT 2-DOOR COUPE

1977 VOLARÉ PREMIER 2-DOOR COUPE

CHAPTER 32

VOLARE (NEL BLU, DIPINTO DI BLU) DOMENICO MODUGNO

Originally released as a single

(Fonit, 1958)

Written by Domenico Modugno and Franco Migliacci

FLYING TOO HIGH CAN BE DANGEROUS, one bad move leads to another, and that move is usually worse than the one before. Committing yourself too early can lead to disaster, but once you go, you go. This song is zooming and whizzing and runs the course, it gets up to speed and barges into the sun, ricochets off the stars, smokes pipe dreams and blasts into cloud cuckoo land. It's a whimsical song and stays aloft.

You get the mental picture, Utopia, and it's painted blue. Oil paint, cosmetics and greasepaint, frescoes with blue slapped on, and you're singing like a canary. You're tickled pink and walking on air, and there's no end to space.

You're the Bobbsey Twins, two minds thinking as one, and it's marvelous and awesome. You get high and you're having a ball everybody's getting a charge out of it, come on let's live a little. It's just a hop skip and jump to cloud nine. You're jetting out and making maneuvers and winging it like an aviator. Mirrored in your own dreams and experiencing a sense of wonder. Flying up through the veil, light as a feather, lingering awhile on the puffy vapors, far above the maddening crowd, the connoisseurs, the judges and cliques. All the organizations, everything that wants to grab at your feet and bring you down to earth.

Around the globe you skyrocket, through the labyrinth. No wonder your happy heart sings. Sings the melodies with all the tonality and vibrations of the senses. Ragtime, bebop, operatic and symphonic. The sounds of violins, it's buzzing in your ears, and it's all in tune, in tune with your mercurial self. You're barnstorming through dimensions. You're on the rim of the universe in the bright lights of the great millennium, nowhere to go but up.

You're fairly certain you have become some kind of biological mutation, you are no longer a mere mortal. You could tear your own body to pieces and throw the bits everywhere. Bending the throttle, climbing high and out of control where everything becomes a nebulous blur, nothing up here but your imagination. You're fluttering and floating, nothing you can't discover, even the hidden things, the deeper you go, the more you can grasp. You try to talk to yourself, but after the first few words the conversation is over. You're blazing like a comet, hightailing it to the stars. Maybe you're crazy but you're no imbecile.

★ ★

THIS COULD HAVE BEEN ONE OF THE FIRST

hallucinogenic songs, predating Jefferson Airplane's "White Rabbit" by at least ten years. A more catchy melody you'll never hear or experience. Even if you don't hear it, you hear it. This is a song that just creeps its way into the air. A song that must be played at weddings, bar mitzvahs and maybe funerals. It's a perfect example of when you can't think of any words to go with a melody and you just sing, "Oh, oh, oh, oh." Supposedly it's about a man who wants to paint himself blue and then fly away. Volare, it means, "Let's fly away into the cielo infinito." Obviously, the endless sky. The entire world can disappear but I'm in my own head.

There is something very freeing about hearing a song sung in a language that you don't understand. Go and see an opera and the drama leaps off the stage even if you don't understand a word. Listen to fado music and the sadness drips from it even if you don't speak a lick of Portuguese. Sometimes you can hear a song so full of emotion that you feel your heart ready to burst and when you ask someone to translate it the lyrics are as mundane as "I cannot find my hat."

For some reason, certain languages sing better than others. Sure, German is fine for a certain type of beer-fest oompah polka but give me Italian with its chewy caramel vowels and melodious polysyllabic vocabulary.

Originally, "Volare" was sung by an Italian singer named Domenico Modugno—just the sound of his name creates its own song. A song that could hit you anytime, day or night. It's always the same. You are always just flying away, higher than the sun.

Bobby Rydell also had a big hit with it. He was a Philadelphia singer from the late fifties—giving rise to the Philly sound. Rydell was either a Sinatra wannabe or a Bobby Darin wannabe. Darin and Rydell more or less both being a high-energy version of Sinatra. You won't hear much Dino influence in either of these guys, unlike Elvis. (Phil Spector in "Be My Baby" took the "whoa, whoa, whoa"s from this song.)

The song is a seduction in Italian beginning with a dreamy little piano vamp followed by Domenico's vocal swathed in organ before the familiar swoop of the title's hook comes in.

The sound of the record is sumptuous, full of disparate elements but never cluttered; a drummer who deftly switches from swinging brushes to the added impact of sticks, dancing pizzicato strings, space-age echoey organ. The vocal is all about dynamics—one moment soft whispers of intimacy, the next joyous exultation, an interlude of recitation followed by wistfulness that translates without language.

CHAPTER 33

LONDON CALLING
THE CLASH

Originally released as a single
(CBS, 1979)
Written by Joe Strummer and Mick Jones

PUNK ROCK IS THE MUSIC OF FRUSTRATION

and anger, but the Clash are different. Theirs is the music of desperation. They were a desperate group. They have to get it all in. And they have so little time. A lot of their songs are overblown, overwritten, well-intentioned. But not this one. This is probably the Clash at their best and their most relevant, their most desperate. The Clash were always the group that they imagined themselves to be.

"London Calling"—there was a stage play of the same name that came out in London in 1923, a musical of treacly skits. But the phrase never died. In the forties "London calling" could only have sinister effects. London calling—send food, clothing, airplanes, whatever you could do. But then, calling is immediate, especially to Americans. It wouldn't be the same as Rome calling or Paris calling or Copenhagen calling or Buenos Aires, or Sydney, or even Moscow. You can pass off all these calls with somebody saying, "Take a message, we'll call back." But not with London calling.

The counterpoint to the song is Roger Miller's "England Swings Like a Pendulum Do," "bobbies on bicycles two by two." The Clash puts this to rest. Phony Beatlemania has bitten the dust. The Clash have nothing but disdain for Beatlemania. The adolescent and extreme emotions of the awkward age. "I Wanna Hold Your Hand," all the theme songs for Little Missy and the school maids, sweet-little-sixteen mania, have no place in the real London anymore. In the real London war is declared. London is in the underworld. The world of drugs and waterfront real estate—the Clash sneer at the fool on the hill. That truncheon thing is going to come down on your head while you are singing "Hey Jude." The engines are broken, and the Clash live by the river.

Any time you mention a river in America you are thinking about the Mississippi. A beautiful, wide flowing body of water that rolls down the middle of America. And everything that that conjures up. The Clash are talking about the Thames. But in America you can't help but think Mississippi. And this is what gives this particular song such broad appeal. All hell is breaking loose, but the guy is still living by the river, which gives him some type of hope, and a way to escape from any difficulty.

"REDUCE TENSIONS
and Sleep Deeply"
PSYCHOSCOPE RECORD #3
33⅓ RPM
R-1359
AN ANSWER TO
sleepless nights
sleeping pills
tranquilizers
eye shades
ear-stoppers
vibrating mattresses?
"SELF-POWER SERIES" by EMILE FRANCHEL
SLEEP DEEPLY TO LIVE FULLY!
Can be used on
"Learning While Asleep"
Equipment, too.
© PSYCHOSCOPE RECORDS
PRINTED IN U.S.A.

CHAPTER 34

YOUR CHEATIN' HEART HANK WILLIAMS WITH HIS DRIFTING COWBOYS

Originally released as a single

(MGM, 1953)

Written by Hank Williams

THIS IS THE SONG OF THE CON ARTIST. In this song you're the swindler who sold me a faulty bill of goods—beguiled me, double crossed me, and now you're out of moves and soon you'll be groaning with prolonged suffering. How do I know? I just know. Maybe I have a crystal ball, maybe I read tarot cards, maybe I just foresee things, maybe I have a sixth sense. A whole lot of maybes. I don't know how I know, I just know.

Your cheatin' heart had unlimited power, was unreliable, corrupt, and treacherous—it was responsible for bringing poison and pestilence into the homes of millions, and you commended yourself for it, you celebrated yourself. You pulled all the strings, acted as if you owned the world, passed the buck, and went back on your word. You were shameless and couldn't be depended upon, you bit the hand that fed you. You were amoral, haughty, and falsified the true doctrines of life, you devour human flesh, but it's all over now, you were caught and found guilty, and all these things can be substantiated by sworn statements. It was hot tips and inside information that did you in, your heart betrayed you, it wasn't what you thought it was. The chickens have finally come home to roost and now it's time to pay, payment's long overdue.

Soon you'll be on a cryin' binge, wide awake and troubled, your consciousness filled with self-disgust. Tears like falling rain, no little drizzle, but sheets and buckets. Rain that soaks up your mattress and bedspread, a trail of tears that go down into the basement, the real wet stuff.

You've robbed me of any possibility of happiness, and for that your mind will punish you. Unable to conk out, even for a minute. You'll bawl and scream and call out my name, but I'll rebuke you, won't recognize your voice—it won't sound like you. You'll want me to swing by, but I won't be doing that.

Soon you'll be marching on the same side of the road as what I'm on, we'll see how you handle that. You were prejudiced, stupid and hypocritical, and now your cheatin' heart is making its presence felt. You didn't want me to live an honest life, you bamboozled me and ripped me off, and now there'll be no more sleep for you. Not this night, not any night. You thought you could do anything, thought you'd live forever, and you gave it all you had. You just didn't have the right character to pull it off. It's a hell of a thing isn't it.

★ ★

THIS SONG CAN BE TAKEN A COUPLE of different

ways. In one, for instance, you're a psychic. You have one of those little stores where you advertise that you read tarot cards or something. Somebody comes in, you throw some cards down and it's easy to see that you are talking to somebody that has a cheating heart and you are just laying it out for them. There's nothing they can do about it. The damage has been done.

A song like this will make you examine yourself—all your actions. It is perfectly played and sung. The fiddle and steel guitar phrases are a great part of the melody. Each phrase goes hand in hand with the voice. This is very hard to do in this day and age. It takes simpatico players and is done with very simple notes of a chord, played with the exact correct intensity that is not alterable. Phrases like this are worth more than all the technical licks in the world. If Hank was to sing this song and you had somebody like Joe Satriani playing the answer licks to the vocal, like they do in a lot of blues bands, it just wouldn't work and would be a waste of a great song.

That's the problem with a lot of things these days. Everything is too full now; we are spoon-fed everything. All songs are about one thing and one thing specifically, there is no shading, no nuance, no mystery. Perhaps this is why music is not a place where people put their dreams at the moment; dreams suffocate in these airless environs.

And it's not just songs—movies, television shows, even clothing and food, everything is niche marketed and overly fussed with. There isn't an item on the menu that doesn't have half a dozen adjectives in front of it, all chosen to hit you in your sociopolitical-humanitarian-snobby-foodie consumer spot. Enjoy your free-range, cumin-infused, cayenne-dusted heirloom reduction. Sometimes it's just better to have a BLT and be done with it.

There's really nobody that comes close to Hank Williams. If you think of the standards that he recorded, and there's not that many, he made them his own. You can imagine him singing all the pop hits of that time, like "How

Much Is That Doggie in the Window," "Que Sera, Sera"—even "Stardust" and "On the Sunny Side of the Street." If he had done all those songs he could have given Sinatra a run for his money.

The simplicity of this song is key. But it's also the quiet confidence of a singer like Hank. The song seems slower than it is because Hank doesn't let the band lead him. The tension between the chug of the near-polka rhythm and the sadness in Hank's voice drives it home. Hank is one of those rare artists that can sing anything and make the song his own. Listen to "On Top of Old Smoky," or "Cool Water."

Willie Nelson would be the only one who could be considered even in the same neighborhood. For instance, he sang the song Elvis had a hit with, "Always on My Mind." All you remember now is the Willie version.

CHAPTER 35

BLUE BAYOU
ROY ORBISON

Originally released on the album *In Dreams*
(Monument, 1963)
Written by Roy Orbison and Joe Melson

IN THIS SONG YOU'VE BEEN SAVING YOUR

pesos, penny pinching all your small change. Working freelance, doing drudge work so you can get back to Blue Bayou. A place close to heaven that lingers in your head. A place you left a half century ago out of curiosity, to see the big world, and put it under your heel.

What you found were long lines of people, people speaking different languages, mumbling unintelligible things. You found the Tower of Babel—you found skyscrapers of gibberish and double talk, superstructures and frameworks of hot air and bullshit. You weren't compatible with anyone, you learned no secrets, didn't get any rave reviews or achieve any success. You never built or rebuilt anything, and now you're sick of it, the flakiness of it—you're sick of playing with yourself and you want to get back to Blue Bayou.

Back to the animal and spirit world, back to that sweet little angel, the girl next door, who you left standing by the gum tree in the wetland swamps. Back to her music, her religion and her culture. You're getting flashbacks from the

past, and you want to go back to all that, before you get carried away too far and are ravaged by time. Back to happier times, where folks are lively and merry, where you can have a blast, make the most of things and clown around. Where you can put both oars in the water and balance yourself. Where you can play with a full deck and the universe belongs to you—where you are the title holder, back to where you can bait your hook, cast your net, sail around on your skiff and be a seadog. Where you can ease off, let up, and master reality and no one keeps tabs on you. Where you can hang out with the minks and muskrats and sit beneath the black willow and the jungle leaves, tune into the sunrise with your sleepy eyes.

If only you could do all that, how happy you'd be, how fulfilled, no more squabbles, you're dreaming now. You'll see your long-lost friends, your bosom buddies from years ago, and when you do, maybe you'll feel like your life has been recovered, that you're out of the woods. You're looking forward to contentment and happiness on Blue Bayou, although right now you're friendless, all by yourself, and feel marooned, ill at ease and edgy. You're pretty much as you've always been, your form has changed but your spirit has remained the same. You're prepared for anything. You're thinking ahead.

★ ★

THIS IS BOTH A SPECTACULAR SONG AND A

spectacular record. They are not always the same thing. Sometimes songs can be slippery in the studio—they can go right through your fingers. Some of our favorite records are mediocre songs at best, that somehow came alive when the tape was running.

This one has it both. The sadness exists both in the words and in the operatic swoop of Roy's voice—it is just about impossible to separate the singer from the song. Linda Ronstadt did a terrific cover version, but it will always be Roy's song.

As a matter of fact, a lot of people cite *The Dickson Baseball Dictionary* as listing "Linda Ronstadt" as a synonym for a fastball because it "blew by you." When Herb Carneal announced a Twins game and the opposing team's batter would take a strike off a fastball, Herb would giddily exclaim, "Thank you, Roy Orbison."

It's also interesting that when this single came out it hit the pop charts and the R & B charts but not the country charts.

CHAPTER 36

MIDNIGHT RIDER
THE ALLMAN BROTHERS

Originally released on the album *Idlewild South*

(Capricorn, 1970)

Written by Gregg Allman and Robert Kim Payne

THIS IS THE MIDNIGHT RIDER, the arch-protagonist. He wears a costume and a mask—the farmer, the small businessman, the law-abiding citizen. In the beginning, he objected to this and that, was told to "be careful with that tongue of yours." So, he went with another weapon—and he's here now to undermine local culture and put it under an iron heel.

He condemns sexual immorality and opposes social corruption. A sworn enemy of political bureaucracy, power brokers, election fraud, decadent union leaders, party hacks, corporate parasites, sugar daddies and other bankrollers. The midnight rider seeks to force disruption and he's got the power and ability to make and enforce the unwritten law. He's the Bull Moose, the Whig, the left wing and the right wing. He is the enemy of all those that prey on the weak and the ignorant, and he represents all people who are afraid to speak freely, and imposes arbitrary authority. The midnight rider wants to return things back to

a pre-corporate economic order and wipe the slate clean. He makes religious hatred a formality. The midnight rider is a figure who uses violence to do good. He's already given you fair warning and he arrives after dark, at bedtime in the witching hour.

The midnight rider has sympathizers.

BLUE SUEDE SHOES

Words and Music by CARL LEE PERKINS

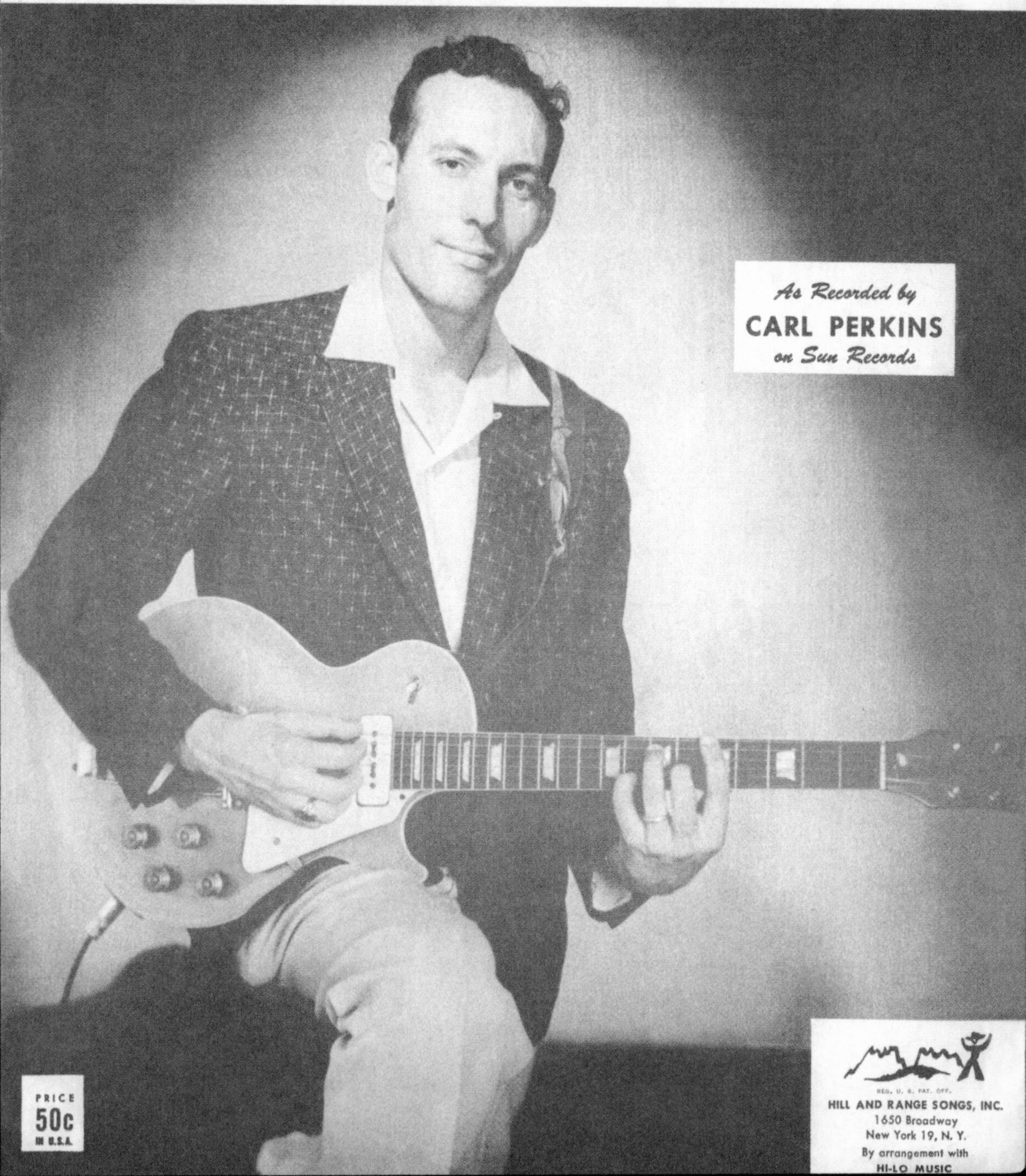

As Recorded by
CARL PERKINS
on Sun Records

PRICE
50c
IN U.S.A.

REG. U. S. PAT. OFF.
HILL AND RANGE SONGS, INC.
1650 Broadway
New York 19, N. Y.
By arrangement with
HI-LO MUSIC

CHAPTER 37

BLUE SUEDE SHOES
CARL PERKINS

Originally released as a single

(Sun, 1956)

Written by Carl Perkins

THIS SONG IS THE HANDWRITING on the wall, loaded with menacing meaning—a signal to gate crashers, snoops, and invaders—keep your nose out of here, mind your own business and whatever you do stay away from my shoes.

You'd like to be on good footing with everyone, but let's face it, there's a harshness to your nature that might go unsuspected and it can be downright nasty when it comes to your shoes. Especially when it comes to your shoes.

Your shoes are your pride and joy, sacred and dear, your reason for living, and anyone who scrapes or bruises them is putting himself into jeopardy, accidentally or out of ignorance it doesn't matter. It's the one thing in life you won't forgive. If you don't believe me, step on them by all means—you won't like what happens.

You get on well with most people, and you put up with a lot, and you hardly get caught off guard, but your shoes are something else. Minor things may annoy

you, but you rise above them. Having your teeth kicked in, being pounded senseless, being dumped on and discredited, but you don't put any weight on that, none of it's as real to you as your shoes. They're priceless and beyond monetary worth.

You can take it all and think nothing of it, torch my walls, steal my loot, ransack my car, turn my house into a towering inferno, but look out when it comes to my shoes, they're beyond measure. There is no price on them, no asking price. Be careful not to scratch them or rub them the wrong way. If you want to live and know how to live, you'll stay off my shoes. You're not talking tough guy stuff, you're just saying what's important and what's not—you can drink my booze as well, suck my vital fluid, swallow it all, bottoms up, one swig after another, drink yourself under the table. But all that to me is so-so and run of the mill, just don't scuff or step on my shoes. Stay away from them, don't be a dummy.

These shoes are potent. They can foretell the future, locate lost objects, treat illnesses, identify perpetrators of crimes, all that and more, and I'm drawing the line when it comes to touching them. They're beyond estimate, worth their weight in gold, and you're being put on notice. Don't step on them, you'll be made an example of—there will be repercussions, I can vouch for that.

These shoes are not like other shifty things that perish or change or transform themselves. They symbolize church and state, and have the substance of the universe in them, nothing benefits me more than my shoes. They answer all my silly questions. I can walk eight thousand miles in them. They're wild and they notice everything. I never walk away and leave them anywhere, and they'll never leave me either.

They neither move nor speak, yet they vibrate with life, and contain the infinite power of the sun. They're as good as the day I found them. Perhaps you've heard of them, blue suede shoes. They're blue, royal blue. Not low down in the dumps blue, they're killer blue, like the moon is blue, they're precious. Don't try to suffocate their spirit, try to be a saint, try to stay as far away from them as you possibly can.

★ ★

THERE ARE MORE SONGS ABOUT SHOES than

there are about hats, pants, and dresses combined. Ray Price's keep walking
back to him, Betty Lou got a new pair, Chuck Willis didn't want to hang his
up, Bill Anderson nailed a pair to the floor and the Drifters got sand in theirs.
Sugar Pie DeSanto sang about slip-in mules and Run-DMC about their Adi-
das. There's songs about new shoes, old shoes, muddy shoes, runnin' shoes,
dancing shoes, red shoes by the drugstore, and the ol' soft-shoe.

Shoes reveal character, station, and personality. Mothers used to advise
their daughters that they could tell a lot about a man by his shoes. In one of
the versions of *The Prince and the Pauper*, the prince is revealed by his shoes,
which he didn't change with the rest of his clothes because he was unwilling to
sacrifice the comfort of his well-made footwear. Cinderella was identified by
the fit of her glass slipper.

Felix Edmundovich Dzerzhinsky, a.k.a. Iron Felix, trusted consort to both
Lenin and Stalin, led the early Soviet secret police organization known as the
Cheka. During the Red Terror, the beginning of the Russian Civil War in 1918,
Lenin asked him how many executions the Cheka was responsible for. Dzer-
zhinsky suggested they count the number of shoes and divide by two.

But for all that shoes revealed, they did not give up their secrets easily. It's
only a recent thing that clothing, including footwear, emblazoned the man-
ufacturer's name upon itself. Workwear often did it—take Levi Strauss jeans'
guarantee of durability, for instance. But the better the clothing, the softer it
proclaimed its lineage. Your foot would obscure the signature on the insole,
and like the Mafia code of omertà there was nothing revealed on the tongue.

Sure, you could walk down Fourteenth Street, or the corresponding bar-
gain mart in any city, and buy a knockoff pair of Pradas, Bruno Maglis, or Stacy
Adamses, but you weren't about to fool the cognoscenti. You didn't need to see
the name to recognize the shoddiness of the workmanship, the vinyl in lieu of

leather, the crimping of the faux alligator. Snoop Dogg would never find the knockoffs on point, much less write a song about them.

When you're young, it's hard to have enough money to have the nicest car in the neighborhood. Or the biggest house. But you just might be able to have the sharpest shoes. They become a point of pride. And worth taking care of.

It used to be that leather shoes were kept spit-polish clean, lovingly cared for with a chamois, oiled and polished after each wearing. It was important to keep them looking brand-new.

One can trace the lineage of virginal shoes in the extreme back to the Chinese practice of foot binding, where pressure is applied to a young girl's feet until they can fit the shape and size of the tiny and traditional lotus shoe, a remarkable and horrible four inches around.

More recently, there was the white buck, a shoe so proud of its immaculate surface that it came with a small brush to buff any blemish from existence. And one can't forget blue suede shoes. Has ever a shoe proclaimed its frivolity more joyously? Has any article of clothing ever said more plainly that it wasn't meant for the farm, that it wasn't made to step in pig shit?

Poor Carl Perkins, watching Elvis Presley sing his song "Blue Suede Shoes" on TV in 1956 from a hospital bed. At that point, Carl's version had sold half a million copies, but a car accident on the way to *The Perry Como Show* slowed the momentum of Carl's career and it never truly recovered. But, perhaps, he was never truly meant to be the king of rock and roll. His ballads, like "Sure to Fall," were achingly beautiful but hillbilly at their heart. Songs like "Tennessee" were certainly worlds away from Chuck Berry's "Promised Land," going so far as to brag that they "built the first atomic bomb in Tennessee." Carl was too much the country boy for the rock and roll crown.

Elvis, on the other hand, was all sullen eyes and sharp cheekbones, backwoods-born but city-livin', truck-drivin', hip-shakin' with a feral whiff of danger. Carl wrote this song, but if Elvis was alive today, he'd be the one to have a deal with Nike.

CHAPTER 38

MY PRAYER
THE PLATTERS

Originally released as a single

(Mercury, 1956)

Written by Georges Boulanger, Carlos Gomez Barrera, and Jimmy Kennedy

---

"MY PRAYER" HAS BEEN A HIT IN FIVE different decades and has been recorded in fourteen different languages. Originally, it was an instrumental crafted in 1926 by a French salon violinist with the title "Avant de mourir," which translates to "before dying." Thirteen years later an American, Jimmy Kennedy, added lyrics, giving the song a new title, "My Prayer." It was a quick hit for both Glenn Miller and the Ink Spots.

This is another one of those songs that comes from a European melody. The twilight part is an intro to the song. A lot of songs written at this time had introductions built into them. If you have two songs and don't know what to do with either one, you slap them together and the results can either be catastrophic or illuminating.

As far as the lyrics go, they seem to have great meaning because the lead singer in the Platters is such an emotional singer. "My Prayer" is a rapture in blue. In most cases a prayer would be for someone to get well, or all the standard things people pray for; maybe a loved one recovering, a family situation which needs to be straightened out. There are 1,001 things to pray for, but a rapture in blue and the world far away, and your lips close to mine, doesn't actually, in the real world, add up to much. Garth Brooks had a song called "Unanswered Prayers," which seems to have more to do with praying than this one does.

Bon Jovi had a song called "Livin' on a Prayer." Also there's "I Say a Little Prayer," sung by Dionne Warwick, but those are merely pop songs. The greatest of the prayer songs is "The Lord's Prayer." None of these songs even come close.

The guy in the Platters, Tony Williams, is one of the greatest singers ever. Everybody talks about how Sam Cooke came out of gospel to go into the pop field. But there's nobody that beats this guy. He took his spirituality with him into the pop world. You couldn't picture this guy getting shot, bare-naked in a motel room.

The Platters don't need back-alley blues full of flatted notes and double entendres, they carry their soul with a cooler-than-thou looseness, offhand and urbane, exuding hipness the way James Dean exhaled cigarette smoke, and they broadcast from a station out among the stars where it is always twilight time.

★ ★

Here are some other pop songs based on classical melodies:

"All by Myself": based on the second movement of Sergei Rachmaninoff's Piano Concerto No. 2 in C Minor, op. 18.

"American Tune": based on a melody line from a chorale from J. S. Bach's *St. Matthew Passion*, heard in part 1, numbers 21 and 23, and in part 2, number 54. Bach's version was itself a reworking of Hans Leo Hassler's "Mein G'müt ist mir verwirret."

"Can't Help Falling in Love": based on "Plaisir d'amour" (1784), a popular romance by Jean-Paul-Égide Martini.

"A Groovy Kind of Love": based on the Rondo movement of Muzio Clementi's Sonatina in G Major, op. 36, no. 5.

"Never Gonna Fall in Love Again": based on the third movement of Sergei Rachmaninoff's Symphony No. 2 in E Minor, op. 27.

"Stranger in Paradise": based on Alexander Borodin's "Gliding Dance of the Maidens," from the Polovtsian Dances in the opera *Prince Igor*.

"Catch a Falling Star": based on a theme from Johannes Brahms's *Academic Festival Overture*.

★ ★

Here are some pop songs with English lyrics based on foreign melodies:

"Autumn Leaves": originally a French song, "Les feuilles mortes" ("The Dead Leaves"), with music by Hungarian-French composer Joseph Kosma and lyrics by poet Jacques Prévert. Yves Montand and Irène Joachim debuted the song in *Les portes de la nuit* (1946).

"Beyond the Sea": originally a French song, "La mer" ("The Sea"), by Charles Trenet. Roland Gerbeau made the first recording in 1945; Trenet recorded it in 1946.

"Cherry Pink and Apple Blossom White": originally a French song, "Cerisiers roses et pommiers blancs," with music by Louiguy and words by Jacques Larue. The song was first recorded by André Claveau in 1950.

"Feelings": originally a French song, "Pour toi" ("For You"), with music by Louis "Loulou" Gasté and words by Albert Simonin and Marie-Hélène Bourquin. Dario Moreno debuted the song in the film *Le feu aux poudres* (1957).

"The Good Life": originally a French song, "La belle vie," with music by Sacha Distel; included in the film *Les sept péchés capitaux* (1962).

"I Wish You Love": originally a French song, "Que reste-t-il de nos amours?" ("What Remains of Our Love?"), with music by Léo Chauliac and Charles Trenet and words by Charles Trenet. The song was first recorded by Trenet in 1943.

"If You Go Away": originally a French song, "Ne me quitte pas," with music and words by Jacques Brel. The song was first recorded by Brel in 1959.

"Let It Be Me": originally a French song, "Je t'appartiens," with music by Gilbert Bécaud and words by Pierre Delanoë. The song was first recorded by Bécaud in 1955.

"My Way": originally a French song, "Comme d'habitude" ("As Usual"), with music by Claude François and Jacques Revaux and words by Claude François and Gilles Thibaut. The song was first recorded by François and released in 1967.

"What Now, My Love?": originally a French song, "Et maintenant" ("And Now"), with music by Gilbert Bécaud and words by Pierre Delanoë. The song was first recorded by Bécaud in 1961.

"Yesterday, When I Was Young": originally a French song, "Hier encore" ("Only Yesterday"), with music and words by Charles Aznavour. The song was first recorded by Aznavour in 1964.

"Sukiyaki": originally a Japanese song, "Ue o muite arukō," with music by Hachidai Nakamura and words by Rokusuke Ei. The song was first recorded by Kyu Sakamoto in 1961.

"Answer Me": originally a German song, "Mütterlein," with music and words by Gerhard Winkler and Fred Rauch. First recorded by Leila Negra and the Vienna Children's Choir in 1952.

"A Day in the Life of a Fool": originally a Brazilian song, "Manhã de Carnaval" ("Morning of Carnival"), with music by Luiz Bonfá and words by Antônio Maria. The song was first recorded by Bonfá and others for the film *Black Orpheus* (1959).

CHAPTER 39

DIRTY LIFE AND TIMES
WARREN ZEVON

Originally released on the album *The Wind*
(Artemis, 2003)
Written by Warren Zevon

THE SONG OF THE WRETCH, the contaminated life—a song that corrupts itself and corrupts others—a deathbed confession. Your free lovin' days are winding down and in the bag. You've lived a life of excess, too much soft living. An obstinate life, unhampered by constraint, you're settling things up and packing it in.

You couldn't tolerate being told what to do, not even if it was for your own good, couldn't endure any command, you had your own ideas. Always liked whores and shenanigans better than hard work and glory, you were full of energy and fucked with horsepower. You were the wise man, the guru, the shaman who wears the toga at the Mazola party. The reprobate with the fancy talk who hits everybody up for whatever they have, telling everybody more than they want to know. You were bad as can be and something awful—fantasy heartthrob of every woman, and the horned bull hero of every man, the mad doctor who sucks the milk of wisdom from the nurses. You're the tomcat with the stiff penis who pisses gold urine and brings ripples of excitement to stodgy old lives, paid your bills with bouncy checks, gives everyone who tries to help you a tongue lashing.

Surrounded yourself with goons and other shitheads, who helped you stay out of jail and that's how things were—that's not even the least of it. You swung from one tree to another, had your bread buttered on both sides, the hell-raiser whose wife wrote you off, but you didn't notice. You were up the street fucking your brains out, with a woman that was hardly anything, on a tiger skin rug, smoking the water pipe.

Now you're looking for the next woman, poorly made, someone with a heart of gold, a real humdinger, pompous and arrogant. Someone to drag you further on into your dingy life. A woman you can cherish and who'll kiss your ass, and if you can't get her you'll get her blood relative. You're as crude as can be, world weary and bored to tears. Your entire life has been too much of a good thing, one orgy after another, depending on how far back you want to go.

Now your body is failing—losing fire and virility—there's an empty space at the center of yourself. You're saying a long farewell to greatness, piling the ashes of your life into the corner. In view of all this you still have the backbone and audacity to look the endgame straight in the eye and carry on with bravado. Untroubled and tough as nails, you're not mournful or morose, you're standing tall, cool, still gritty and filled with spunk. You're lifting up a life that's been shot full of holes, going for broke this time, undaunted and unafraid.

This is a song with head turning beauty. This is a daredevil of a song.

★ ★

THIS IS A GREAT RECORD, but it's not the Warren we usually

know from "Werewolves of London" and things like "Poor Poor Pitiful Me."
This is a different voice, but just as authentic. Listen to the harmony vocals
on this record. They sound like they are being done in somebody's kitchen.
Totally unrehearsed and funky as ever. You don't hear harmony voices like this
on too many records. It is a hell of a performance and that includes everybody playing on it. Not one note misplaced; from the guitar player to the bass
player. The content of this song is what it's all about and it's delivered in its
most accurate way.

The braggadocio, the swagger and strut of early Warren is long gone. But
unlike in most cases where that's all the guy's got to give and when that's gone,
he's gone, Warren still can get it out there. He shows you the other side and it's
just as strong.

The braggart, the roué, the ironic observer, and the inebriated fool were
all roles Zevon chose to play in his songs. And possibly at times in his life. But
stripped to the bone, as in this song, the artistry jumps out at you like spring-
loaded snakes from a gag jar of peanut brittle.

Being a writer is not something one chooses to do. It's something you just
do and sometimes people stop and notice. Warren was a writer till the very end.

But the writing part only was there to serve his brilliant piano playing. In
other words, Warren's lyrics and piano playing were two parts of the same thing.

That's Ry Cooder playing here, and Ry Cooder is a man with a mission.
There was no road map when he was trying to figure the connection between
Blind Lemon Jefferson and Blind Alfred Reed, the place where conjunto met
the gutbucket blues, where even a jake-leg could do a cakewalk.

Ry lived it and breathed it, learning at the feet of the masters and carrying
the knowledge like seeds from region to region. He improved every record he
ever played on and many that he didn't.

CHAPTER 40

DOESN'T HURT ANYMORE
JOHN TRUDELL

Originally released on the album *Bone Days*

(Daemon, 2001)

Written by John Trudell

THE SONG OF THE SUFFERER, one that penetrates to the heart of the matter.

Your desire and imagination are wearing thin, and the longer your lifeline is, there's less guarantee that either will hold up. You question everything about yourself, but you don't know what you're questioning—renounce and relinquish all your thoughts, thoughts that crash into a heavy cloud of fog—thick as a brick wall, splits into a million pieces and goes missing—powerful thoughts that explode like the big bang.

In this song there's a million ways to go mad, and you're familiar with them all, you just don't talk about it and even if you did, your words would be difficult to catch. You try to invoke memories of friendship, but they can't be found—searching in rooms where abandoned ambitions have stacked up. Vacant rooms, rooms where the most brilliant minds you've ever known have been cut up and reassembled. You don't have a civil word for anyone who speaks to you, and your sense of being has been shut off. All things have come to a sudden conclusion, you're embracing ghosts, pursuing shadows—you've been the victim of destructive energies. Heaved thunderbolts and boulders at Time, but Time persisted. Your heart's been roughed up, damaged and it's out of action, but it's not spurting any blood, so you don't recognize or even subscribe to the hurt. There must be someone who will listen.

Where do you go? How do you identify with a world that has set you aside, a world that took everything from you without asking, a world that's asleep, bedded down and deep into slumber-land taking one long endless siesta. You'll go into the mythic land of rebirth, stare up into the mirror of the night sky and talk to your ancestors. They're wide awake.

★ ★

YOU CAN GO UPRIVER OR DOWNRIVER. You

need a landmark on the shore—a tree or a rock—to know if you're moving at all.
Pirates sail on the open sea and feel like they're standing still. Everyone judges
history from where they are standing. It's the only way they can make sense
of it. Otherwise it's too intense. That's why people constantly draw connec-
tions with what has come before. They say those who do not know the past are
doomed to repeat it, but those who obsessively footnote it are just as doomed
to repeat it endlessly.

There's a difference between imitation and influence. And then there's
something else entirely. Like John Trudell.

His story is quite violent. John was a Santee Dakota Indian born in the
early forties in Nebraska. The Santee Dakota Indian territory went from the
plains of Minnesota to Montana. Eventually the government herded them all
into a tiny strip of land someplace in Nebraska where John grew up. He grew
up on the reservation and went to the local government school and then went
into the navy. When he came out he saw all the treaties between the white man
and the Indian had been broken and he had the knowledge, sensibility, and
morality to actually do something about it.

He went to broadcasting school and was able to use that in his spoken-word
performance early on. He was at the head of the United Indians of All Tribes
group that took over Alcatraz, setting up a radio station there in 1969 and taking to the airwaves on KPFA.

In the midst of it all he got married, had three girls and a pregnant wife
besides. At the same time, he became more of an activist in Indian affairs. This
was all during the Vietnam War and civil rights protesting so a lot of Native
American dissent went under the radar.

The treatment of the Indians was a long-forgotten issue in America, especially on the front pages. With the Black unrest and anger in the streets, the
condition of the Indians in America could be overlooked. It is the most horrid

of all mistreatments. There's a place in Mankato, Minnesota, commemorated by a plaque in the town square, where forty Santee Dakota Indians were hung in the 1870s.

Sometime in the late seventies, John led a demonstration of various tribal people in Washington on the steps of the Capitol. A day after that, his trailer home in Nevada on the Duck Valley Reservation was firebombed and a padlock was put on the outside of the door. John's pregnant wife and three kids and mother-in-law were burned alive. The arsonists were never apprehended. This gives you an idea of what's deep down in the heart and soul of many of the songs that John would write.

The thing about life is it keeps on going even after the headlines stop. John lived into the new century and kept writing poems. He speaks poems to music—music, which is always a real band playing real instruments. Whatever record he's making, his band can do it all, from rock and roll to melodic melodies in back of him—anything which serves the tone of his voice and his poems. There's an ancient spirit coming through him and a person can understand it. His words carry in their simplicity the confidence of ancient wisdom.

He's no rapper. More like an ancient Greek poet; you know exactly what he's saying and who he's saying it to. John faced the same government that Sitting Bull faced—a government that wanted to kill him with either guns or disease. Just get rid of him altogether and take his land away. He stood alone, and now that he's gone he stands even more alone, never a commercial success.

John was not mainstream. He didn't talk about popular subjects like hustling drugs, pimping, and materialism, glorifying those things. John's music can elevate you and usually does. Maybe there isn't a place for that. John Trudell was not the kind of Indian to put on a headdress and be a star in Buffalo Bill's Wild West Show. He was no cigar store Indian, and he wouldn't have identified with "Kaw-Liga." People who go on nonstop about civil rights, women's rights, gay rights, animal rights and on and on need to take a look at what America has done to the people who were here from the beginning.

Take a moment—read a little more about John Trudell than what is offered here. He deserves it. And after you do, seek out his music. A good place to start would be the *AKA Grafitti Man* album, full of simple direct performances with John accompanied by his Oklahoma soul brother Jesse Ed Davis.

As you get deeper into his work, you can't go wrong with the *Bone Days* album and a song called "Doesn't Hurt Anymore." The space between it and Hank Snow's song "I Don't Hurt Anymore" is profound. One is sort of a gaudy statement about teardrops drying, but the other will tear your heart out.

In a real sense the only thing that truly unites us is suffering and suffering only. We all know loss, whether you're rich or poor. It isn't about wealth or privilege—it's about heart and soul, and there are some people who lack that.

They have no landmark on the river's bank to show them how fast they are traveling or where they are heading. And the saddest part is, they will never be able to hear John Trudell.

CHAPTER 41

KEY TO THE HIGHWAY LITTLE WALTER

Originally released as a single
(Checker, 1958)
Written by Big Bill Broonzy and Charles Segar

IT'S IRONIC, A LOT OF DIGNITARIES GIVE YOU

the key to the city. That indicates that everything in the city is open to you for inspection at any time. I have gotten lots of keys to different cities but I've never really tried to inspect anything yet. Seven keys from seven houses in seven towns are supposed to cure impotence. A new key is better than an old key. You can strike a werewolf in the forehead with a key and that will bring him back to his human form. If you are ever fired from a job, you've got to give your keys back. Some people say that if you take the last nail out of any coffin, it will work as a key to unlock whatever you want to unlock.

Little Walter is an excellent guitar player and in a lot of people's opinion a greater singer than anyone on Chess Records. He is an amazingly flexible singer, totally believable on teen-themed pop-blues tracks like "Too Late," "One More Chance with You" and "I Got to Find My Baby" (with the immortal line "I'm gonna walk the floor baby till my moustache drag the ground").

But he also turns in what is perhaps the deepest vocal in the whole Chess catalog on the song "Last Night." Unadorned, with no histrionics—controlled, nuanced and true; a seamless mesh of harmonica and voice. Little Walter always sings effortlessly, he always keeps his cool and underplays everything. His records are soothing and refined.

He's also known as the electric blues harmonica originator, the master craftsman and the prime mover. But this record makes it clear he was all that and more.

Little Walter could take other people's ideas and make them his own. "My Babe" is a good example of that. "My Babe" has been around for ages as a gospel song called "This Train." Walter changed the words and made a classic performance out of it.

"Key to the Highway" is an update of a Big Bill Broonzy song. But Bill's is a blueprint for what Walter does with it. The key to the highway is the key to the cosmos, and the song moves in and out of that realm. The key is the key that gets you out of the city. A city gets smaller and smaller in the rearview mirror, in your memory a city you're happy never to go back to. When Walter sings, "I'm going back to the border where I'm better known," he means it. He's had enough of Michigan Avenue and Lakeshore Drive and the Sears Tower.

Little Walter did not call himself the Back Door Man and he didn't dig nineteen-year-old chicks. Out of all the artists on Chess he might have been the only one with real substance. He could make anybody sound great. He was never meant to reach old age.

CHAPTER 42

EVERYBODY CRYIN' MERCY
MOSE ALLISON

Originally released on the album *I've Been Doin' Some Thinkin'*
(Atlantic, 1968)
Written by Mose Allison

IN THIS SONG YOU'RE HEMMED IN, going round and round the loop, doing full turns—empty-headed, blind to where you're going and stumbling through the dark. You're loaded to the rafters, smacking, and slapping at things, buttoned down, no holds barred, going nonstop in a direct line, and everybody's patting you on the butt.

You're on the spine-tingling roller coaster over there at the amusement park. Thumbing a ride on the Ferris wheel, shooting ducks and winning kewpie dolls, while all of mankind cries mercy—every race, creed, and color—rich and poor, from all quarters, from all over creation.

Funny thing you're detached from it all, scoffing at everything you see, giving no credit, to whatever you hear. You're being diplomatic, ask no favors, take people at their word, and you want to be treated the same. Even if you goof up, you're not going to be one of those miserable rascals with his knees in the dust

begging for mercy. You're not a crybaby. You have no idea what the proper definition of the word is anyway. Whatever is going to happen, is going to happen, so let's just get on with it.

This song is all about hypocrisy. Hitting and running, butchering and exterminating, taking the grand prize and finishing in front. Then being big hearted, burying the hatchet, apologizing, kissing and making up. It's about the hustle.

You're high principled, chivalrous and Mr. Respectable, Mr. Don Juan, but you don't have to pretend with me. You're the spoofer, the playactor, the two-faced fraud—the stool pigeon, the scandalmonger—the prowler and the rat—the human trafficker and the car jacker. Take your pick and be selective and be honest about it. You're the hardliner for fair play and a square deal, just as long as you've got your irons in the fire and enough on your plate. Muckraking, chaos and bedlam, you're a party to it all.

Strangely enough, you find the lack of justice intolerable and the lack of mercy even more so. It sets you off, and you wonder if it's even possible in this world. Even handed justice, tempered with the milk of human kindness, the divine light of mercy, the kind of mercy that signals a new beginning. You like to praise it and put it on a pedestal, almost worship it, but it has no place in your life as long as you're employed. Whatever your racket, your shit job, whatever your routine task is, you never had it so good, so let's leave justice and mercy to the gods of heaven. Better to go to the local movie theater, be a movie goer, sit in the opera—some wacky farce, some silly bull-crap stage show, or better yet stare at a crack moving down the wall. Think about kindness and benevolence, giving people a second chance.

This song says let's be just and honorable to the point of our natural ability.

Let's not make empty gestures, or expect people to let up on us, let's not expect to be pardoned or forgiven. Mercy may be a trap for fools.

★ ★

AN INTENSE AND SERIOUS TAKE ON HYPOCRISY

in the real world by the great Southern gentleman, blues/jazz giant Mose Allison. Like peeking through a knotholed fence and seeing the world for what it is. "Have Mercy Baby," "Mercy Mercy Me," and "Sisters of Mercy." The word mercy comes from the same Latin root that the word mercantile or merchant comes from. It's hard to see the connection, but Mose does. That's why he slips in "just as long as it's business first." Have mercy, you say to the judge. Temper it with mercy. Give a cheer and get your souvenir. Life is a sideshow.

Mose sings this song in his usual style. Laid-back, half asleep. Like you don't want to spend any energy. It's too hot and humid. It's sung in a lazy way, disguising the important intent. Mercy is a word that has almost been exempted from common speech. Tough guys show no mercy. A song that goes beyond social commentary, it's a facet of human nature that we don't really want to know. Well you don't have to go to off-Broadway to see something plain absurd, just open up your eyes and walk down the street. Yes, indeed. A lot of jazz chords in this song—augmented thirds and fifths, lots of passing chords that Mose can't do without. Listen to the way Mose sings his vowels, and you'll see how it's connected.

This song could easily be the skeleton of the monster that is "Ball of Confusion." Each of these songs offers a jaundiced view of the current state of the world—both when the songs were written and, sadly, now. But where the Tempts sang a frenzied jumble of words exploding from the center of the fray, Mose is the bemused detached observer of a few extremely carefully chosen words, resigned to our foolish foibles but unwilling to let them pass without comment.

CHAPTER 43

WAR
EDWIN STARR

Originally released on the album *War & Peace*
(Gordy, 1970)
Written by Norman Whitfield and Barrett Strong

IT'S INTERESTING TO POINT OUT THAT THIS

song was originally an album track by the Temptations on their *Psychedelic Shack* LP from March of 1970. There was some clamor to put it out as a single but the savvy marketing men at Motown were hesitant to offend the portion of the Tempts' fan base who hadn't yet made the transition to producer Norman Whitfield's politically charged psychedelic soul sound. By this time the Motown Sound had definitely crossed over to white audiences, but it also had a large and surprisingly conservative Black middle-class audience. As recently as two years earlier both of those contingents were well serviced by the Temptations' *Live at the Copa* record, which featured versions of standards such as "Hello Young Lovers," "The Impossible Dream" and the Irving Caesar and George Gershwin composition "Swanee," alongside a handful of their own hits.

Edwin Starr was an ambitious second-string artist at the label. He'd only had one hit since signing and was still looking to make his mark. He was in the enviable position of having no fan base to alienate and could do as he pleased. He approached Whitfield and suggested that he re-record "War." Smart move. Starr's version of the song was more aggressive than the Temptations' version and full of Whitfield production flourishes. The single came out three months after the *Psychedelic Shack* LP and hit the number one position on the *Billboard* Hot 100. It defined Starr's career, helped modernize Motown's voice and sold over three million copies, helping give the lie to the song's lyrics.

One can't help but wonder whether or not the peacenik sentiment behind the song was sincere or merely the next relevant subject to be mined in the attempt to reach Young America's wallets between "Agent Double-O-Soul" and "Mercy Mercy Me (The Ecology)." Even if it was a blatant exploitation of the peace movement, it's still a stronger song than "Eve of Destruction."

Wars need a clear message, a striking image that can fit on a recruitment poster, a slogan, a rousing anthem that can be sung in marching cadence. Vietnam, on the other hand, was a small war, fueled by hubris and murky to the citizenry, who were left unsure what they were fighting for.

Historically, great nations do not fight small wars. As far back as seventh-century Greece, when there were over fifteen hundred independent city-states, the rules of battle were already drawn hierarchically. Back then you wouldn't see a larger city attack a small outpost somewhere. Battle is seldom a powerful nation's first resort.

"War, what is it good for?" Perhaps that is the wrong question. Perhaps the better one is the one that Country Joe McDonald asked when he put words to Louis Armstrong's "Muskrat Ramble" and asked the other question everybody had about Vietnam, "What are we fighting for?" War is a powerful weapon, sometimes the only choice for two parties who have exhausted all other options. When negotiation and diplomacy fail, it is often the only solution.

Wars have raised people, freed them from oppression and actual slavery. Wars have reopened trade routes and channels of communication. And just as history is written by the winners, so it is with war. The winning country will tell you what has been gained. You have to look to the losers to find the atrocities. Or listen to the dissenting voices.

In the early thirties, two-time Medal of Honor recipient Smedley D. Butler retired from the Marine Corps, where he had served as a major general. He toured the country giving a speech that was published first by *Reader's Digest* and then in book form. The speech, titled "War Is a Racket," painted a picture of profiteers pouring gasoline on the flames of battle to boost their bottom line. He confessed to his own actions on multiple battlefronts that hurt large numbers of people to ensure profits for a very few.

It's clear that one answer to the question posited in this song is the bottom line. Which is appropriate seeing as this song was co-written by Whitfield along with the man who gave Motown its first hit, that oft-covered anthem of avarice—"Money." "War" obviously filled the coffers at Hitsville USA but, then again, war was usually good for business. As the organizer and president of the Brotherhood of Sleeping Car Porters Asa Philip Randolph said in 1925, while Smedley Butler was still serving in the military, "Make wars unprofitable and you make them impossible." But war is about more than money. It's about rights. Property rights to be specific. Who owns the land and the oil beneath it?

But as much as wars attract privateers, rounders, rogues, international rapscallions, mercenaries, and profiteers, money-lust is not the only path to war. There is also pomposity and pride. Wars have also been started out of xenophobic fear over incursions both real and imagined. There were religious wars like the Crusades and wars as tools to consolidate sprawling rebellious empires like the Peloponnesian War. People fought wars to expand their borders or to defend them. They fought for vengeance and to extend the domain of their flag. And in 1838, Mexico and France went at it when King Louis-Philippe discovered that an expatriate pastry chef named Remontel had not received reparations when his Mexican café was ransacked by looters.

Some may argue that there are better reasons to go to war than an unpaid patisserie bill. But war has always contained a machismo whiff of futility.

Nowadays, it's not the inciting incident but the nature of war itself that has changed. There was a time when the leaders of opposing armies could be found on the battlefields. And they would have to face down their enemy and test their opponent's mettle with the conviction of their own belief. The steel in the spine and blade determined the victor.

One mark of civilization is the ability to increase the distance between yourself and the person you kill—the blade gave way to the gun, which gave way to the bomb, which gave way to any number of long-range killing machines. The more powerful you were the further you could be from the action. The most powerful were half a world away, snug in their bathrobes while nameless soldiers did their killing. Plausible deniability helped these warmongers sleep, with arrogance born of distance and an ignorance of specifics they believed kept their hands clean.

There is a sequence in the documentary *The Fog of War* where former secretary of defense Robert McNamara discusses his and General Curtis LeMay's role in firebombing sixty-seven Japanese cities during World War II before the bombings at Hiroshima and Nagasaki. In a single night, one hundred thousand men women and children were burned to death in Tokyo on McNamara's recommendation. It forced LeMay to admit, "If we had lost the war, we'd all be prosecuted as war criminals." For the rest of his life, McNamara wrestled with the question "What makes it immoral if you lose but not if you win?"

The simple answer sounds glib—history is written by the winners. The bigger problem, though, is that in modern warfare, unwinnable battles are being fought on multiple fronts for no clear purpose—a mishmash of ideology, economics, fearmongering, and chest-beating. Whole sections of the globe can lie seemingly calm for long periods of time only to suddenly erupt unexpectedly with disruptive explosions like some sort of geopolitical herpes.

In the third act of *The Merchant of Venice*, the jester Launcelot tells Jessica that the "sins of the father are to be laid upon the children." Many people try and make the same argument about the only presidential dynasty we have had so far and the two Gulf Wars, which caused such far-reaching ripples on the waters of history.

The Father, witnessing the possible end of the Cold War but facing greater instability in the Middle East and skirmishes even closer to home in Panama, needed a sure hand overseeing the three-dimensional chessboard the world had become. He was swift and surgical in responding to Saddam Hussein's aggressive invasion of Kuwait. There were casualties, to be sure, but lower than any would have predicted, and when the battle was over the Father's approval rating was 89 percent, the highest in Gallup poll history. And perhaps most important, the United Nations raised sanctions against Iraq and established a commission to guarantee they would not revive their weapons of mass destruction program.

This is what was laid at the Son's feet, not sins. But the Son was not the man the Father was and in the wake of post-9/11 paranoia and failed attempts to break up the "Axis of Evil," the Son turned his attention to Iraq. His eye was not as clear, nor his hand as steady, as his father's. Claims were made about weapons of mass destruction which were never found, battles were fought on many fronts. Lives were lost in the course of an invasion that was not provoked.

If Robert McNamara and Curtis LeMay were alive they would know what to call the men who sent those soldiers to war. But the blame doesn't end there.

As a people, we tend to feel very proud of ourselves because of democracy. We walk into that booth and cast our votes and wear that adhesive "I Voted" sticker as if it is a badge of honor. But the truth is more complex. We have as much responsibility coming out of the booth as we do going in. If the people we elect are sending people to their deaths or worse, sending other people half a world away—whom we never even consider because they don't look like us or sound like us—to their deaths and we do nothing to stop it, aren't we just as guilty?

And if we want to see a war criminal all we have to do is look in the mirror.

CHAPTER 44

BIG RIVER
JOHNNY CASH AND
THE TENNESSEE TWO

Originally released as a single

(Sun, 1957)

Written by J. R. Cash

WELL-MEANING PEOPLE CAN SUFFOCATE YOU

with praise. Johnny Cash loves being the Man in Black and dresses accordingly, but the truth is he is much more of a well-rounded artist and man. His best records are playful and full of wordplay and humor, miles from the august solemnity of the murder ballads, hardscrabble tales and Trent Reznor covers that his fans came to expect. Songs like "One Piece at a Time," "Get Rhythm," and the chart-topper Shel Silverstein wrote, "A Boy Named Sue."

Johnny Cash gets this song from Woody Guthrie's "The Biggest Thing That Man Has Ever Done." Lines like "I built the Rock of Ages, 'twas in the Year of One." "I'm the man that signed the contract to raise the rising sun." "I was straw boss on the Pyramids, the Tower of Babel, too." He just takes off from there. "I taught the weeping willow how to cry, and I showed the clouds how to cover up a clear blue sky."

The key element to this song is the chain-gang thump of the acoustic rhythm guitar. You can't really cover this song properly leaving that behind. The released recording is maybe the biggest thing Johnny has ever done. The song is built on the call-and-response guitar part played on acoustic guitar. The guitars are doing this kind of chomping along with the beat. There's a shadow phrase and an echo phrase like a chain-gang thump. Like somebody chopping a piece of wood.

If you get Johnny Cash's *Essential Sun Collection*, you can hear a few versions before they came up with the final one. Some of the lyrics are different and they don't have that call-and-response part together yet. It's a great example of how songs evolve in the studio.

Johnny Cash is a gospel singer, or he thinks of himself as one. Somewhere along the line, he turns into Gargantua, Finn MacCool, Jigger Jones all in one. He could climb across rivers. He could lay track and take down greenhorns. He's a teller of tall tales—parts the clouds and drinks nitro. This is the real Johnny Cash, and "Big River" is his theme song.

CHAPTER 45

FEEL SO GOOD
SONNY BURGESS

Recorded by Sun Records, 1957/1958—unreleased

Written by Herman Parker Jr.

IN THIS SONG YOU'RE FEELING AS GOOD AS

can be, and don't need to be convinced.

You never felt better, and you have a hunch you're going to feel this way for the rest of your life.

You're rockin' steady with nerves of steel, laid back, and you're going like the wind, gonna boogie night and day. Like a rainy day, like a downpour, dripping and drenched with your clothes all soggy. All the cats and jokers, the whole body politic, all the earthlings, every stripe and color—you're taking their guts out and serving them for dinner—you're intensely alive, coming through the kitchen, and you're rockin' narrow and hard, rockin' to the point where no one can hardly see you anymore, like the Zephyr Queen, like the Panama Flyer, rockin' steady and shaking the earth—breaking and entering, unworried about your dreams.

This song takes the sting out of life, everything you see you're snapping it up and they're forking it over. You're freed up and going flat out.

You're the boogie man, the menace from outer space, bloody, neat, and sharp like a surgeon's scalpel—kingly, soul deep in the eyes of the world. You're flying low and got your landing lights turned off. You're gonna boogie on back to where it began, to the birth of creation, unlock the laws of the universe—bone shaking and burning liquid fuel, you're lathered up, electrified and leaving nothing un-licked. You're the lavender leading man, the black sheep, perfect gentleman in a tailcoat and you got a gal who's sky high, stretched out and wild, two-faced beauty, your gold-digging showgirl, full skirted in a cocktail dress. Wolf-bait on mescaline, your catty just folks' gal and she's breathing down your neck.

You're in everybody's bedroom pulling the wires, parting the curtains of whatever's hidden inside—following nature and banging out the chords. Doing the hopscotch boogie, the rhumba boogie, the heel and toe boogie—attacking the mystery of the sun, everybody boogies. Moms and dads, old timers and has-beens. Schulberg, Gauguin, Picasso and Little Miss Muffet, they all boogie, but nobody boogies like her and you. You're tapping out the rhythm, saving your best for last, seeing with your third eye, you and your flame throwin' femme fatale. Playin' and sweatin' at the Models Ball, at the wife swapping scene. You're gonna boogie to the limit, plain as day with obvious intent, hard core and clinging to life, stiletto sharp. Denver after dark, Las Vegas, Honolulu too, all in a straight line. Physical beauty and an intellectual attraction is what it is and it's out in the open.

This song is greedy from the word go, and fearless like crazy. This song takes the sting out of life, everything you see you're snapping it up and they're forking it over. You're freed up and going flat out. Hunting the beast, it's as simple as that. This song is always the newest and latest thing, never looks for what it doesn't have. There's nothing important that it's missing. You're gonna boogie till they're all dead. This is tip-top rock and roll at its finest, in pure form. In the halls of the Rock and Roll Museum it would reign supreme and unrivaled if it was only in there.

IF YOU WANT TO HEAR A POLITICAL RECORD,

play this one. Put it on repeat, play it over and over, night and day, and maybe if you're wondering what happened to the late, great country you grew up with or how you can make America great again perhaps this record can give you some idea. But whatever you do, keep your windows shut and don't tell anybody, most especially your friends, that you're playing it unless you want them to judge you.

This is a record of extremes, more black than black, more white than white. There was no name for this kinda thing in the fifties, so nobody knew how to sell it until the Cleveland disc jockey Alan Freed purloined the term "rock and roll" from a bunch of earlier risqué records, Black and white country boogie and rhythm and blues, both sides of the fence using the same term as a thinly veiled euphemism for copulation. Needless to say, once a name like that was attached, selling the music became a whole lot easier.

Of course, this was before America was drugged into a barely functioning torpor. Sure, the seeds of abuse were sown as so-called wonder drugs rolled out of the labs and into the streets. Truck drivers discovered white crosses and black beauties, helping them deliver truckloads of perishable produce cross-country without sleep, keeping America fed while putting a little something extra in their paychecks. Meanwhile their wives took the edge off with the soporific effects of Librium and Miltown, soon to be immortalized in the Jagger-Richards song "Mother's Little Helper."

The use of drugs went from casual to cavalier and soon even the legal prescription drugs couldn't meet the demand. And there were plenty eager to fill the need. If you're wondering how a nation will fall, look to the drug dealers. Drug dealers in every city with bull's-eyes on their backs, daring anybody to shoot them.

No one wants to see their city in that kind of picture but it's always hard to recognize yourself in someone else's photo. Mankind's first sense of

self-awareness was a reflection in a stream, and then a mirror. The eventual view we get in a photo, and then Skype, Zoom, and FaceTime—where we see ourselves as others see us, without the image reversed as in a mirror or stream or in the plate glass of a window as we cross the street—seems somehow wrong, perhaps opening the door for deepfake imagery and other unreality.

It's probably lost to the sands of time whether Sonny Burgess came to this song himself or if canny Sam Phillips recycled a Little Junior Parker Sun record in the same way he did with "Mystery Train" for Elvis Presley. His records could only be made by a sweaty, sinewy band that played behind chicken wire night after night in a series of off-the-highway bucket-of-blood joints.

This is the sound that made America great.

CHAPTER 46

BLUE MOON
DEAN MARTIN

Originally released on the album *Dream with Dean*
(Reprise, 1964)
Music by Richard Rodgers
Lyrics by Lorenz Hart

THIS IS THE DINO THAT ELVIS imitated. The lazy, good-for-nothing drunk. "Blue Moon"—the daddy of doo-wop although there's not a drop of doo-wop in it. Anybody can play and sing it. It's a song you start out with if you are playing popular music. It's a song that's hard to do anything different with, although plenty of people have tried. Some of the versions of the song defy belief. I think Elvis and Phil Spector both tried their hand at it. Elvis never did do it in person. It's one of those songs that makes a good record but it's too much work to make it believable in live performance.

Its appeal is in its mysteriousness. A melody right out of Debussy. Out of nowhere, a form appears before you and you hear a voice whisper, "Please adore me." And then you turn around and the moon has changed color to gold. When's the last time you saw a golden moon? The song makes no sense but its beauty is in the melody.

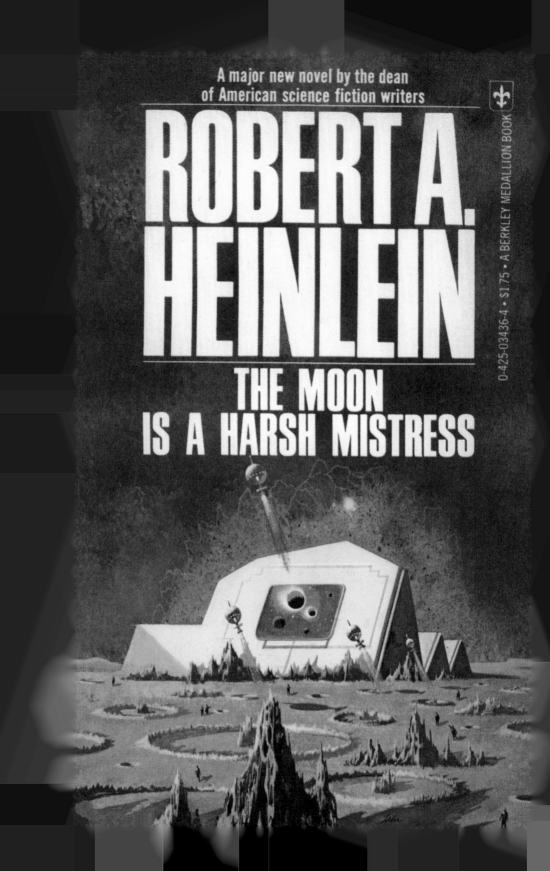

A major new novel by the dean
of American science fiction writers

ROBERT A.
HEINLEIN

THE MOON
IS A HARSH MISTRESS

0-425-03436-4 · $1.75 · A BERKLEY MEDALLION BOOK

This is another song where an inanimate object takes on a life of its own. A variation of the phrase "once in a blue moon." An esoteric term for the moon that probably happens once in a lifetime. "Once in a blue moon." Bill Monroe wrote "Blue Moon of Kentucky," which Elvis did along with a clippity-clop version of "Blue Moon" . . . channeling Dino, which takes everything full circle.

When Elvis did "Blue Moon of Kentucky" he did the same thing he did with "Mystery Train." He souped it up. He took midtempo songs like "Blue Moon of Kentucky" and "Mystery Train" and even "Good Rockin' Tonight"—stripped them down and sped them up. Which is why they called him the

"Atomic Powered Singer." Atomic energy was coming in and Elvis was riding the crest of that.

There's some tape of Dean Martin live at the Sands Hotel at the height of his career made obviously in the hopes of putting out a live album. Listening to the first of two nights, you can't believe that Dino got through the set. Words dissolve into runs of vowels without the traffic lanes of consonants. Songs start and drift off after a chorus, to be interrupted with a series of non sequiturs and jokes, sometimes at the same time. ("Frank doesn't like anybody to talk during his shows. I don't care if you talk during my show. I wouldn't care if you bowled.") He's funny and charming and plowed.

And then you listen to the second night. A couple of jokes were different. He hit a couple of the releases on songs differently but the two shows were damn near the same. Maybe he really wasn't drunk at all, but he perfected the art of portraying it.

Not for Dino was the hiccupping buffoon nor the buttonholing argumentative drunk. He wasn't the aggressive masher, or the angry devil with rage set free by liquid courage, spoiling for a fight. Anything but.

Dean was the lovable roué, everybody's beloved uncle, charming and soused with a bit of mischief in his eye and a good-time gal in his bed. He was drinking without hangovers, lust without penalty and the man both Sinatra and Elvis wanted to be. He died broken, sad and alone—drunk for real in a stained windbreaker, alone in a restaurant off the Sunset Strip with red leather banquettes and amber liquor. Both he and the restaurant had seen better days.

Dino sings deceptively. You can't hear any effort, you can barely hear any breathing. There're little slurs and modulations that are as hard to sing as they are easy on the ear. In the bridge, he hits a blue note and then a line or two later ("I heard somebody whisper, please adore me") there is a little waver in his voice that brings to mind Nick Lucas, Tiny Tim's mentor, who sang the original "Tip-Toe Thru the Tulips."

Some songs, like "Yes! We Have No Bananas," "When I'm Sixty-Four," "North to Alaska" and "Free Man in Paris" are as dependent on their arrangement as the music or lyrics for their identity. Not so "Blue Moon." "Blue Moon" is a universal song that can appeal to anybody at any time.

The song has traveled through time and crossed every cultural abyss. It has been country crooned and soulfully invoked. It is a cornerstone of doo-wop and a springboard for jazz improvisation. Pop singers have swung it and sung it nonstop since it was written.

It is a love song, by turns devoted and wistful. The simplicity of the lyrics makes it universal with enough detail to rescue it from being generic. The malleability of the song frees it from being too associated with any single version and allows it to belong to everyone.

Compare, for example, Dino's version with Elvis's dreamy take or Bobby Blue Bland's uptown blues with a Latin tinge. Made for wildly different audiences, but the beauty of the melody and the poetry of the lyrics become available for everyone.

It's the dignity that is within this melodic ballad that gives it its class and greatness.

CHAPTER 47

GYPSIES, TRAMPS & THIEVES
CHER

Originally released as a single
(Kapp, 1971)
Written by Bob Stone

THIS IS A SONG ABOUT BEING ON THE MOVE

and keeping it moving—being born on the move. The grand tour, one town a jumping-off place to the next—no dead ends. A who, whodunit and a who cares kind of song. You never go where you're not wanted, and once you're there you never refuse to leave. Never a greeting or parting word for anyone, and nobody ever prevents you from returning. Whatever it is, if it's not your business you'll make it your business.

You've evolved over thousands of years and you're still traveling through, setting up the tent and making ends meet. Hoaxes, tournaments and spectacles, that's your line of business. Drugstore cowboys, girl watchers, night owls—everybody and their uncle, you lighten them up and bleed them with ease. You give nightmares to people while they're fully awake. People whisper behind your back—lampoon you, satirize, mock and ridicule you, make bitchy comments but your place in the sun is secure. You're the sexual companion of lunar spirits, and you can make otherwise ordinary people do completely pointless and horrifying things, you've got life down pat.

The man you call Grand Daddy was on the move too. Grand Dad peddled slinky lubricants that treat anything from gall bladders to constipation, arthritis, rheumatism and relieves sluggishness—harangued every Tom, Dick and Harry with the hard truth of the gospel—fire and brimstone sermons, lake of fire rhetoric, moved people to undergo religious and political conversions, now he can't see beyond his nose and doesn't have enough sense to come in out of the rain. Soon he'll turn into a butterfly and his bones will fly away.

People of no ethical background for you are easy prey, and they're your line of business—patronizers, snobs and highbrows, whoever they think they are.

But you understand them as geometrical bodies, with solid angles and planes, and you know how to make them see wonderful things, and you can make music that drives them mad. You've got the character of Saturn and the spirit of Venus. Passion and desire, you give it to them under the counter. Your guidelines are simple, and you rule nothing out. Strip yourself bare and dance the sword dance, buck naked inside of a canvas tent, fenced in, where the town royalty, the top brass and leading citizens, bald as eggs throw their money down, sometimes their entire bankroll.

Floaters and pickpockets is what some people say. Crossbreeds and bastards is what others say. But they don't know their ass from their elbow, the things they put up with, you wouldn't tolerate for a minute. There's never been a day when you haven't woken up and said that this wasn't going to be a good day.

It's a family thing. Cousins, half-brothers, aunties, grand uncles, nieces, cousins twice removed, a fraternal order and sisterhood, an enclosed circle is what it is, a secret society. Your heart is where your seat of wisdom is, there's no

gray matter in your brain, you're always leaving the door open to friendship. You look in the mirror and see a confidante—you're never inaccessible to yourself. Your philosophy of life is wait and see. You make anybody who sets their eyes on you feel like they're falling in love, you've got a long lineage—and you go everywhere at all times. This-a-way, that-a-way, over the hill, around the mountain, up the road and down the road, can you go past the cutoff point—sure, go where you like.

★ ★

WE ARE GOING TO SKIP THE CARNIVAL. This

is about a pregnant gal. In the old days, we used to say "knocked up." This is
Tanya Tucker picking up somebody just south of Mobile. She's got a mama and
a papa who are very violent and a grandpa who is a con man. It goes right in line
with who she is—a sixteen-year-old who is now knocked up. This song takes
place on the dividing line between the old culture and the new. Probably one
of the last traveling medicine shows. Maybe like Oral Roberts or something.
Scooping up money and whatnot. Oral Roberts, the old Oklahoma preacher.

Gypsies, tramps, and thieves could easily be the answer to the question,
"Name three types of people you'd like to have dinner with." It depends what
you're eating, doesn't it? Then again it doesn't really matter what you're eating,
all that matters is who you're eating with.

The tarnished-angel myth is a hard one to buy into. It's much easier to
imagine Little Egypt doing her dance of the pyramids. At least it seems like
she was having fun beguiling men.

Cher had a difficult childhood. Her biological father left when she was just
nine months old. Her mother went on to marry another five times.

This song is a thinly veiled metaphor for her father/mother relationships.
Eventually Cher met and fell in love with Sonny Bono, an aspiring singer and
actor. Sonny was a record producer, a protégé of Phil Spector's, and went on
to have great success singing with Cher. But his greatest achievement was as
a congressman, where he helped pass the Sonny Bono Act, which extended
copyright terms for all songwriters.

This song melts everything down, browns it up and deep-fries it—it'll milk the cow till it gives blood.

CHAPTER 48

KEEP MY SKILLET GOOD AND GREASY UNCLE DAVE MACON

Originally released as a single
(Vocalion, 1924)
Written by Uncle Dave Macon

THIS IS A BLAST FURNACE OF A SONG AND

it climbs all over you—smokes your meat and steals your brain—and it's free with the bottle. The Grand Daddy of all cooking shows—a real pot boiler. Greased-up, well oiled, slippery as can be and ready to sizzle.

In this song your self-identities are interlocked, every one of you is a dead ringer for the other. You're the Dalai Lama, the Black Monk and the Thief of Baghdad all rolled into one, and the whole world is your city. You're prowling and shoplifting, going down the East End, back where you came from, to the wilderness and brush—back to Chinatown and Little Italy—saddlebags full of barley and cornbread, rosemary and ivy, and sides of bacon in your pocket. You're unmuzzled and unleashed, nightwalkin' up the crooked way, the Royal Road, stealing turkey legs and anything sweet and spicy, roaming through the tobacco fields like Robin Hood, broiling and braising everything in sight.

Putting everything in an open-faced sandwich and washing it down with plum brandy. Every day you wake up—you ask yourself, will you keep puttin' your hand to the plow, your shoulder to the wheel, will you keep on flogging yourself to death just to make a living—no you will not, that's over with.

You're tearing up the earth and kicking up dust and people are out for you. Sharpshooters, snipers, ogres stampeding after you, but you're not worrying your head over it, not shrinking from any of that, and not in awe of anyone. You're gallant under fire—got bulldog courage. Multiracial, bisexual, celibate, scrambled together from sheet metal, copper and wrought iron, doctored up with butterfat and vinegar, and they're no match for you, you'll emasculate them, strike them dumb and put them under the concrete. You're freethinking, broad minded, combining pleasure with truth, and speaking in heart-to-heart talk—fucking and farting your way through blind alleys with prunes and castor oil—throwing all the weenies and liverwurst into the frying pan, and you're tasting everything. Maybe someday you'll slow down, take off your shoes, unbuckle your belt, go on leave, but not now.

You're Long John Silver and you've got snakes in your boots, fortune cookies and glazed doughnuts, and you're drinking iced coffee—eating dried beef and picnic ham, swallowing whole mouthfuls of Boston cream pie and jelly roll like a pastry chef, got the whole food chain and you're gonna open bake it, barbecue it all to perfection.

You're the hash-slinger with the red-hot griddle, every minute of every day at every point in time. You corner the market, hammer out deals, do business with everybody. You've got the gun that helped win the west, surefire self-protection, and the impulse to fire it. Hitting dimes tossed in the air, shooting cigarettes out of your girlfriend's mouth, getting her drunk on Canadian whiskey and sangria, turn her into a boozehound. You're licking your chops, looking at whole piles of scamps—the street bully, the freeloader, the

PORK CHART

RETAIL CUTS OF PORK - WHERE THEY COME FROM AND HOW TO COOK THEM

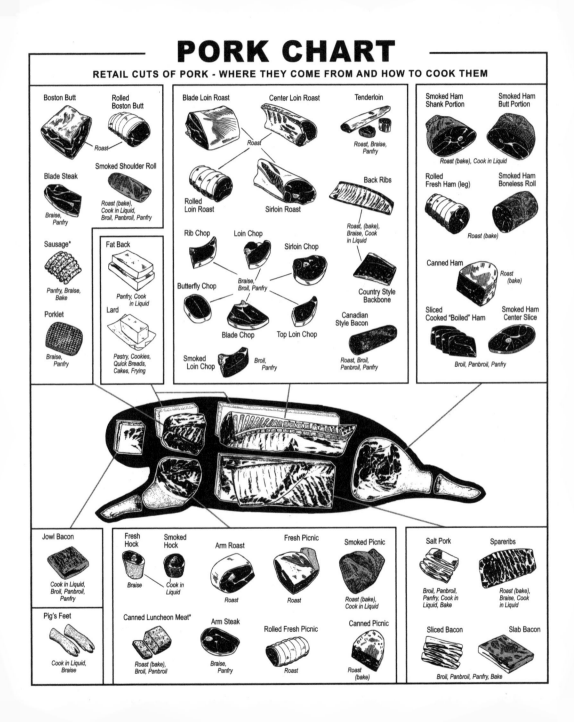

Boston Butt

Rolled Boston Butt

Roast

Blade Steak

Braise, Panfry

Smoked Shoulder Roll

Roast (bake), Cook in Liquid, Broil, Panbroil, Panfry

Sausage*

Panfry, Braise, Bake

Porklet

Braise, Panfry

Fat Back

Panfry, Cook in Liquid

Lard

Pastry, Cookies, Quick Breads, Cakes, Frying

Blade Loin Roast

Center Loin Roast

Roast

Rolled Loin Roast

Sirloin Roast

Rib Chop

Loin Chop

Sirloin Chop

Butterfly Chop

Braise, Broil, Panfry

Blade Chop

Top Loin Chop

Smoked Loin Chop

Broil, Panfry

Tenderloin

Roast, Braise, Panfry

Back Ribs

Roast, (bake), Braise, Cook in Liquid

Country Style Backbone

Canadian Style Bacon

Roast, Broil, Panbroil, Panfry

Smoked Ham Shank Portion

Smoked Ham Butt Portion

Roast (bake), Cook in Liquid

Rolled Fresh Ham (leg)

Smoked Ham Boneless Roll

Roast (bake)

Canned Ham

Roast (bake)

Sliced Cooked "Boiled" Ham

Smoked Ham Center Slice

Broil, Panbroil, Panfry

Jowl Bacon

Cook in Liquid, Broil, Panbroil, Panfry

Pig's Feet

Cook in Liquid, Braise

Fresh Hock

Smoked Hock

Braise

Cook in Liquid

Arm Roast

Roast

Canned Luncheon Meat*

Roast (bake), Broil, Panbroil

Arm Steak

Braise, Panfry

Fresh Picnic

Roast

Rolled Fresh Picnic

Roast

Smoked Picnic

Roast (bake), Cook in Liquid

Canned Picnic

Roast (bake)

Salt Pork

Broil, Panbroil, Panfry, Cook in Liquid, Bake

Spareribs

Roast (bake), Braise, Cook in Liquid

Sliced Bacon

Slab Bacon

Broil, Panbroil, Panfry, Bake

prostitutes' pimp, you'll give them all a deadly bite—smoke 'em and steam 'em, you got it all going from the ground up. London broil, rump steak, leg of lamb, you're heating and reheating it all like a short order cook. Drumsticks, hush puppies and gizzards, everything in sight, you're grilling it up and barbecuing round the clock, going house to house and street to street, you keep passing the torch from one hand to the other.

This song is like a silent movie—no irregularities, nothing quick nothing slow, it shows what it has. This is a unified song, all things in constant motion, contiguous, continuity of form, it follows no line, and one part can easily be replaced by another part. It's rakish, stately, proud and defiant—got its finger on the trigger holding a tight grip, got its pinky on the billy club. Flapjacks and hotcakes, green onions and iceberg lettuce, and it's so hot you get a third-degree burn. This song melts everything down, browns it up and deep-fries it—it'll milk the cow till it gives blood. This song is a spirit guide and will act as an interpreter in foreign lands.

★ ★

THIS SONG PREDATES ROCK AND ROLL BY

about thirty years. What's it all about? It's about the happy wanderer, the chicken thief. Bluegrass groups do this, but the song is really not effective unless you repeat the word time three times. Like Uncle Dave does. That's kind of what makes it work. The song is a good example of why talking is not like singing. You don't say to someone "Come here, here, here," or "I'm gonna do that, that, that." You can sing it though and it makes plenty of sense.

Sometimes people ask songwriters what a song means, not realizing if they had more words to explain it they would've used them in the song. This song is all about the repetition—all the time, time, time, home, home, home.

The repetition gives structure, like a trellis under a vine, letting the rest of the song wander where it might. Two lines in the first verse, one in the second, third, and fourth, then two again, then one, and finally three. Structure shifts, words and phrases are invented—a ham of meat. Fell on the hog with all his grip. Characters come and go—who is Mandy and why does she drink, is she the same gal as the shanty owner, who is the man on the log? None of it matters because the singer's skillet is good and greasy all the time, time, time. And what does that mean? It seems like some kind of sexual boast but the song is not an extended sexual metaphor. Rather, there is cooking and theft, drinking and cavorting, bloodhounds and hogs. It is a series of snapshots, random images that summon up a larger whole.

This song follows its own rules, regardless of what you think or don't think. It has nothing to do with Aristotle's logic. "Baby, if you tell me not to work, that's good enough for me. I won't work no more." Uncle Dave jammed phrasing in all over the place, and he was doing it way back when. Try to sing the last verse of this song without jamming phrasing in all over the place.

This is Chuck Berry years before Chuck first duck-walked. The invention of language, from "ham of meat" to "coolerator," is evident in both. The blip/zip of gun to bullet is echoed in the "bolt of thunder and streak of heat" in Chuck's "Jo Jo Gunne."

How different is this from Kristofferson's "He's a walking contradiction, partly truth and partly fiction." Is it the same message for a different audience? Or as Sly would've said, "different strokes for different folks."

So, is Uncle Dave Macon rock and roll? No more and no less than Chuck Berry. But that's not why you listen to either. That's just the bag you put them in. The reason you listen is because, in some way, it sounds like home, home, home.

The song is related to the talking blues. It's like Walt Whitman if he was a musician. The song contains multitudes. It's also played with a resonator on the banjo. It rings and twangs like an electric guitar. The guy is a thief. He steals meat, he steals chickens and he gets his women good and drunk. People say about entertainers that they may sing and play okay, but they are not good people. This song tells you why.

CHAPTER 49

IT'S ALL IN THE GAME
TOMMY EDWARDS

Originally released as a single
(MGM, 1958)
Music by Charles G. Dawes
Lyrics by Carl Sigman

CARL SIGMAN WROTE THE LYRICS TO THIS

song, but the melody was written at least forty years earlier by Charles Dawes, who later on went on to become vice president under Calvin Coolidge. It's not unusual for politicians to write melodies and songs—Jimmie Davis did it with "You Are My Sunshine." That practice continues, right up to the present time, when used-to-be politician Mike Huckabee also writes melodies and is an accomplished bass guitarist. Both Nixon and Truman played classical piano. And Bill Clinton can play tenor saxophone. Lyndon Johnson was supposed to have entertained himself by playing the harmonica.

Anyway, Carl, a lyricist of high caliber, wrote lyrics for melodies or translated many foreign songs, turning them into American hits. Carl wrote the incredible mystical lyrics for the song "Ebb Tide." Tommy Edwards was a rhythm and blues singer, singing the same genre as Little Willie John or Joe Williams.

Either of those guys could have sung the song and made it a hit. It's got eighth notes, pounding on the piano, which drives the song. Extremely subtle for a ballad. In its day, you could slow-dance to it or jitterbug. The arrangement is key. You will not hear arrangements like this these days. It is way thought out, with a real live echo chamber on the vocalist, and layered with counterpoint parts on the strings, and communal voices filling in the gaps. But nothing gets in the way. Back then, the arrangers' names weren't put on the songs, so we have no way of knowing who arranged the song. But it was someone who certainly would take no backseat to Nelson Riddle and such.

The guy Dawes served under, Calvin Coolidge, makes an appearance as a character in Randy Newman's "Louisiana 1927." There, Silent Cal goes to the bayou to witness the carnage. Here, Cal is way behind the scenes after inviting Charles Dawes to be his running mate. Given the ribbing of ineffectualness that the office of vice president has always received—our first vice president, John Adams, described it as "the most insignificant office that ever the invention of man contrived or his imagination conceived"—Dawes had plenty of time to work on songcraft.

Carl wrote the lyrics forty years after Dawes wrote the melody, and Tommy Edwards had the hit seven years after that. Sometimes a song needs to find its time. Other times you have to get it in the street the next day.

As for the game of love, sometimes if you are a spectator or onlooker you can understand or see a game a lot better than the people who are playing it.

CHAPTER 50

A CERTAIN GIRL
ERNIE K-DOE

Originally released as a single

(Minit, 1961)

Written by Naomi Neville, a.k.a. Allen Toussaint

ERNIE K-DOE IS THE GUY YOU WANT TO KNOW

and be associated with. The man knows how to keep a secret. He's not telling anybody anything. You don't have to worry about him spilling the beans behind your back or collecting money for something that he knows about you. Or stabbing you in the back. Not giving anybody any information. Not a stool pigeon, not a sneak, not a snitch. You can trust this guy. The guy who won't tell you his girlfriend's name is the guy you want on your side.

As opposed to the Beatles' "Do You Want to Know a Secret." This is the guy you need to avoid. Not only do you not have to force information out of this guy, but he's just gonna give it to you, whether you ask for it or not. This is a guy who can't keep his mouth shut—could either get you killed or you're gonna have to kill him in order not to get killed.

CHAPTER 51

I'VE ALWAYS BEEN CRAZY
WAYLON JENNINGS

Originally released as a single
(RCA, 1978)
Written by Waylon Jennings

THIS IS A SONG WHERE YOU'RE GIVING SOME

hard-earned advice to the woman who's thinking about giving her heart to you. You're being honest, on the up and up, you don't want her to have the wrong idea about you. In other words, you may be too good to be true, you're being candid and want her to be certain that you're the one for her, but you're not sure she knows what you're getting at.

You've got a complicated past, been snagged and shackled for missteps, human error—wrongdoing and fool mistakes, a lot of screwups. Even been in a lineup and picked out for felonies that you didn't commit, captured for things you had no part in. You're trying to shield this woman and be as authentic as possible, switch the light on in her head about who you are. Not bragging or boasting about anything in your life, or self-advertising yourself. You're just trying to tell her that even though you've done some shady things, and some shady things have been done to you, none of it's been deliberate or premeditated.

It's just that your life has been anything but smooth sailing. You're not squawking about it, you're just trying to warn her, that giving her heart to you might be a calculated risk.

You're not going to turn any corner or turn over a new leaf—you have no motive to do that, you're just trying to protect her and demythologize yourself, at any rate you're hard to classify. Are you a person that should be hailed and applauded for the things you've done, or put down and called dirty names, you're really not sure. You want her to know all that—know what she's getting into.

Most men wouldn't talk to a woman this way, a woman who's thinking of falling in love with him, but you're not most men. You've always been different, a strange duck—mad as a hatter, but you've never been not all there.

In this song you might be getting ahead of yourself—giving an explanation to someone who's never asked for one.

★ ★

SOMETIMES SONGS SHOW UP IN A DISGUISE.

A love song can hide all sorts of other emotions, like anger and resentment. Songs can sound happy and contain a deep abyss of sadness, and some of the saddest sounding songs can have deep wells of joy at their heart. This one can be looked at in a couple of different ways. At first glance it hinges on craziness and insanity. This seems to be a typical logical fallacy—the archetypal distinction without a difference. But let's dig deeper. Suppose Waylon was on trial for murder and this song is Waylon telling his lawyer that he does not want to use the insanity plea when going in front of the judge. He'd rather be crazy and just take it like a man. The insanity plea would cut him off from the world.

When Eddie Cochran recorded his song "Nervous Breakdown" in the late fifties, he had no way of knowing that, when heard through modern ears, it would be deemed politically incorrect. Nowadays, nervous breakdown is a laughably broad term for a panoply of conditions, and the individual peculiarities of the human condition are sliced as thin as a serving of potato during the Great Irish Famine of the 1840s. Which some people will, no doubt, also view as politically incorrect caricature even though the potato was a cheap staple of the Irish population and was decimated by a fungus that destroyed half the crop in 1845.

Of course, knowledge is a good thing but one of the potentially dangerous side effects is that as the field of knowledge gets wider our skin is stretched thinner. People try different ways to insulate themselves as their nerves are rubbed raw—there are various mood-altering substances, some self-prescribed, others classified by the government and only available by prescription. None of these are precise—they are more akin to buckshot than to a sniper's bullet. And though they can be helpful, anyone who has hunted with a shotgun will tell you, you might enjoy the rabbit but you're gonna spend a certain amount of time biting down on buckshot.

Therapy works for a lot of people, though entertainers have it easier than most. Instead of having to pay someone an hourly fee to feign interest in listening to them drone on about their lives, a canny performer can reel in an audience, unburden themselves, and receive adulation as well as a nice payday simultaneously. What issues was Elvis working through with thousands of teenage girls calling out his name? What death issues was Screamin' Jay Hawkins coming to terms with, charging people to watch him emerge from a coffin?

Entertainers understand that a good story is a basic commodity, one they are not about to give away. The therapist is on the wrong side of that transaction—if you have a lurid story to tell, like you want to fuck your father or want to make love to your mother, why are you paying a shrink to listen to it? He or she should be paying you.

Of course, the public has an insatiable hunger and what was salacious yesterday is ho-hum today. What was once a recipe quickly becomes a formula or—as happens both in music and in ditch digging—what started out as a groove quickly becomes a rut.

People begin acting out to have better stories to tell, to not disappoint their audience, whether it be a thousand teenage girls or a solitary therapist. And that's where it moves from craziness to insanity.

I don't know about a lot of performers but I'm willing to take Waylon at his word. He might be crazy, but in no way do I think he's insane.

CHAPTER 52

WITCHY WOMAN
EAGLES

Originally released on the album *Eagles*
(Asylum, 1972)
Written by Don Henley and Bernie Leadon

THE WITCHY WOMAN is the homeless woman, the woman with the world view—the progressive woman—youthful, whimsical, and grotesque. The woman from the global village of nowhere—destroyer of cultures, traditions, identities, and deities.

The lips of her cunt are a steel trap, and she covers you with cow shit—a real killer-diller and you regard her with suspicion and fear, rightly so. Homely enough to stop a clock, she's no pussycat. Appears in wigs, artificial eyes, jewels and cosmetics. T-shirt, shorts and hip boots, fur coat and granny glasses—slate black hair and lips like fine wine—rubs her middle finger against her thumb and sparks fly. There's something about her that you can't shake, could be the uppers and downers, goofballs, hydroxy steroids or gold heroin. Whatever it is it's got you hooked and you seem to be casting a deadly shadow. She's turned your eyes the color of blood and your skin beet red. She's the ancient frog who

There's something about her that you can't shake, could be the uppers and downers, goofballs, hydroxy steroids or gold heroin. Whatever it is it's got you hooked and you seem to be casting a deadly shadow.

sees with her nose and smells with her tongue—she knows what makes you tick, calls you Dickhead, one-eyed Willie or Humpty-Dumpty.

The old coot's got a volatile spirit, banished everything sacred and pure from your life, and regresses you to a childlike state. She's hot as pepper, foul-tasting, she's one crazy bitch, made you a prisoner of your inner demons.

Let me tell you brother, better watch yourself. You were once a diamond in the rough, had a clear conscience and clean hands—now you're a self-admiring, unchivalrous worthless fellow with an evil nature—the scum of the earth and she's had it up to here with you. What are the odds you'll survive? You'll have to forget your manners, stop being polite and put on the skin of a lion.

This is a song that's hard to go with. It's about spirits in the air. It's cheerless and grim—puts ashes in your mouth.

★ ★

IN 1954, BOB LUMAN WROTE, RECORDED, AND

released a rockabilly B-side titled "Twitchy Woman" on the Imperial label. It has remained one of his lesser-known songs. Eighteen years later, Bernie Leadon and Don Henley removed the first letter from the title and launched Henley's songwriting career with lyrics describing a hallucinogenic amalgamation of succubus and thaumaturge, equal parts troubadour temptress and Jazz Age casualty, conjured up partially by reading the Nancy Milford biography of Zelda Fitzgerald in the throes of a flu-driven fever dream.

I wonder why no one has ever removed one more letter and recorded a song about an itchy woman.

Witchy women, witch queens, and just plain old black-magic women have never fared too well in song. Peter Green wrote of one who had him so blind he could not see, who was trying to make a devil out of him. It only barely cracked the Top 40 in the UK but when Carlos Santana covered it, he took it all the way to number 4.

Marie Laveau, the witch queen of New Orleans, was the first member of her bloodline born in America outside of slavery and lived as a free woman on St. Ann Street, walking distance from Lake Pontchartrain, where she presided over ceremonies and celebrations that made use of her skills as a clairvoyant, mystic, healer, and good person to know if you wanted to lay a curse on someone. She'd probably be forgotten today if not for ardent dissenters who published editorials in the New Orleans daily broadsheet the *Picayune*, with impassioned attacks calling her "the prime mover and soul of the ignoble Voudous."

Madame Laveau laughed off the attacks, a savvy enough businesswoman to know that the notoriety would only increase the demand for her specialized services and poultices, one of the first examples of product branding extant. But I doubt even the prescient Miss Laveau could have imagined her popularity, reaching from her death in 1881 to a thriving tourist attraction and associated souvenir industry here in the twenty-first century.

She has been celebrated in a number of songs, perhaps most memorably by Redbone and Bobby Bare. Both are good but I gotta give Bobby the nod, with lyrics by Shel Silverstein about a black cat's tooth and a three-legged dog.

But the shops lining Bourbon Street with the witch queen's name offering talismans and blessed chicken's feet were not the first to capitalize on fear and the unknown. In Salem, Massachusetts, a series of trials based on the accusation of witchcraft were held. These trials involved religion, politics, and gender issues. There was extremism on both sides, people fabricated facts and ignored due process of the law. There were deaths. And today on that location people sell tickets and souvenirs, dress up for re-creations and snap pictures of each other.

So, by the time Bernie and Don wrote their song, the second Eagles single, everybody had an image of what a witchy woman was in their mind. Raven haired, sparks flyin', moon-eyed shadow dancing with crazy laughter. We all know her. And if we mistook Zelda's absinthe spoon for a coke spoon, that was fine. After all, it was 1972. Witches were using different potions by then.

CHAPTER 53

BIG BOSS MAN
JIMMY REED

Originally released on the album *Found Love*
(Vee-Jay, 1960)
Written by Luther Dixon and Al Smith

YOU'RE THE BIG BOSS MAN, THE MASTER OF

the house with a reputation for being cheap and stingy. You're the famous Chieftain, the enormous tight fisted penny pincher who treats all the workers like errand boys. You hold the purse strings and walk the corridors of power—the despot who rubs the print off a dollar bill.

Modern man is your employee—servile and hypocritical, he's the informed citizen, the rational being, the yes man and the ass kisser, and his temple is the movie theater. He's working for you round the clock, and he's dehydrated. It would take oceans of water to cleanse him from his previous lives. He needs rivers of poetry and music, but you won't let him pause or stand down for a second from his chores. Labor unions, uprisings, revolts, empty threats—you don't pay attention to any of that, you let that all go, you're above it all. You're the Cyclopean giant—you're on the right side of history. The supreme oligarch, the Generalissimo, the over-the-top Overlord who treats the whole world like butlers and chambermaids. You're a man of distinction. You should be happy that people want to emulate you.

★ ★

JIMMY REED, THE ESSENCE OF electric simplicity. You

can play twelve-bar blues in hundreds of variations and Jimmy Reed must have known them all. None of his songs ever touch the ground. They don't stop moving. He was the most country of all the blues artists in the fifties. He is slick and laid-back. There's no city concrete beneath his feet. He's all country.

Jimmy Reed is about space. About air being moved around the room. You feel like you can see the light hitting the dust as it swirls under the sway of music. You put him with Jimmie Rodgers and Thelonious Monk, two other musicians whose work never sounds crowded no matter how many players are there. Some musicians are like muscle cars—not Jimmy Reed, he's just happy that the seats are comfortable and the radio works.

No Chicago blues, nothing sophisticated, light as a feather, flies through the air and rolls on the ground. When they say rock and roll, the roll part belongs to Jimmy Reed. If he's not in there, you can't think of it as rock and roll. One of his songs even says, "Let it roll." And he knew what he was talking about. "You've got me runnin', you've got me hidin', you've got me run, hide, hide, run anyway you wanna, let it roll." Yeah, Jimmy.

He plays the harmonica through a neck rack. And you can't do too much with a harp in a neck rack. But he found a way to pull it off and even today he can't be imitated. Every song has the signature harmonica run; it signs off on everything just like Jimmie Rodgers's yodel. It's the same thing really. Little Walter, as great as he was, would be out of place on a Jimmy Reed record, as would Jimi Hendrix. There's no place for that on a Jimmy Reed record. It would even be hard for Keith Richards to find something to do.

Jimmie Rodgers and Jimmy Reed. They got a lot in common besides their name. Jimmy's wife, that's Jimmy Reed, had a lot to do with his songs too. She's probably writing them as he's singing them. And it sounds like they're both doing it off the top of their heads. You can hear her plaintive voice on most of Jimmy's records. She never overshadows him. Same thing for Jimmie Rodgers's wife.

She doesn't sing with him, but she helped him write a lot of his great songs.

CHAPTER 54

LONG TALL SALLY LITTLE RICHARD

Originally released as a single
(Specialty, 1956)
*Written by Enotris Johnson, Robert Blackwell,
and Richard Penniman*

LONG TALL SALLY WAS TWELVE FEET TALL.

She was part of the old biblical days in Samaria from the tribe called the Nephilim. They were giants that lived back before the cataclysm of the flood. You can see shots of these giants' skulls and such. There were people as tall as one-story buildings. They've uncovered bones of these giants in Egypt and Iraq. And she was built for speed, she could run like a deer. And Uncle John was her counterpart giant. Little Richard is a giant of a different kind, but so as not to freak anybody out he refers to himself as little, so as not to scare anybody.

OLD AND ONLY IN THE WAY CHARLIE POOLE

Originally released as a single
(Columbia, 1928)
Written by Charlie Poole and Norman Woodlief

THERE'S A MOMENT EARLY ON IN Billy Wilder's 1951 film *Ace in the Hole* where hard-drinking, harder-living reporter Chuck Tatum, played by Kirk Douglas, is driving to cover a local snake hunt outside of Albuquerque. Tatum has drunk himself down the rungs of journalism from prestigious big-city broadsheets to small-town penny savers. En route, he tells wide-eyed boy photographer Herbie Cook (Robert Arthur) the secret of a good story. He tells him that a thousand rattlers in the underbrush isn't a news story. Even if they get loose, it's too big a number. But as the snakes get captured, public interest begins to swell. And as the countdown gets closer to zero, it doesn't matter that it's less dangerous, it's the fact there is still one out there that preys on everyone's mind. And when there's only one left, nobody can turn away from the story. The kicker, he tells Herbie, is that a smart journalist would have that last snake hidden in his desk so he can control both the story and the audience.

That's the thing about numbers, if they're too big they just become abstract. Being a trillion dollars in debt means nothing when we follow the news, but if you're ten bucks short on rent, it sure gets your attention. It's why war movies are difficult to make. It's difficult to dramatize the immense number of deaths during Stalin's Great Purge but an individual's story during wartime, any war, can be riveting. The metonymic storytelling of Private Ryan, Sergeant York, Colonel Kurtz, Patton, Schindler, and Spartacus make for better films than ones that try desperately to portray only the scope of conflict.

Things happen. Fires, earthquakes, or viruses hit and often the elderly are among the highest in casualties. Huddled together in nursing homes, with compromised immune systems or perhaps unable to flee on withered legs from shooting sprees. The numbers are high even when there are no extenuating circumstances. Old people die and until it's someone closely related, the world just looks at these deaths with detachment, just blips on the actuary table.

Confucius spoke of filial piety, respect for one's parents, saying in his *Analects*: "Few of those who are filial sons and respectful brothers will show disrespect to superiors, and there has never been a man who is respectful to superiors and yet creates disorder. A superior man is devoted to the fundamental. When the root is firmly established, the moral law will grow. Filial piety and brotherly respect are the root of humanity."

This is why Asian cultures treat their elders with such respect—except for possibly the Japanese, whose mythical custom of *ubasute*, carrying the aged or infirm to the top of a mountain to die, was dramatized in Kinoshita's 1958 film *The Ballad of Narayama*. Or India, where involuntary euthanasia of the elderly, or *thalaikoothal*, is practiced to this day.

Actually, if you google the word senicide you'll see that many parts of the world have a push/pull relationship with their older members—the push of veneration, the pull of elimination. The United States with its chrome-plated dreams of spit-shine modernity was never much for the admiration of its senior citizens. Way before taunts of "Okay, boomer" and the calling of people with experience the pejorative term "olds," this country has had a tendency to isolate the grizzled dotard, if not on an ice floe then in retirement camps where they could gum pudding and play bingo away from the delicate eyes of youth.

It would be easy to blame the sixties, with silly slogans like "Don't trust anyone over thirty" or even sillier movies like *Wild in the Streets*, where anyone over thirty-five is herded in camps and given mandatory doses of LSD.

In July of 1928, banjo player Charlie Poole went into a New York studio with guitarist Roy Harvey and fiddle player Lonnie Austin to record "Old and Only in the Way." Now, there are plenty of other songs about aging—it's a pretty regular theme treated both seriously, as in Dock Boggs's "Oh Death," or humorously, as in Wynonie Harris's "I Feel That Old Age Coming On." And there are even those that fall somewhere between, like Orson Welles's 1984 recitation "I Know What It Is Like to Be Young (But You Don't Know What It Is to Be Old)."

John Prine captured the loneliness and despair of aging in his "Hello in There" and as good as that song is, and it's quite good, it is still a song written by a younger man, one full of empathy, who views advanced age as a thing that happens to someone else. And Joni Mitchell's "The Circle Game" tells a story about a boy whose dreams are dashed at age twenty but hopes there will be brighter days ahead. It's supposed to be optimistic but if your dreams are fulfilled at twenty, what do you do with the rest of your life?

Poole's lyrics are incisive and inclusive. He points out the eternal truth that in youth, the oldest among us are viewed as an impediment. We honk our horns at their slower driving, mock their lack of technological savvy and their reduced hearing and sight. But Poole in his prescient bridge points out that old age is waiting for all of us, as surely as the grave. Those who dodge the grave long enough to become eminent will soon discover they are now old and in the way.

It took a certain amount of wit for Jerry Garcia to name one of his side projects, a long-running bluegrass band, Old and in the Way. One thing Jerry knew was his place in the universe. When he formed the band he couldn't have been further away from either thing in the song's title, being a youthful thirty-one years old and the leader of another very popular band. But even then he knew youth and fame were fleeting and Charlie Poole's words resonated for him.

He knew, as the great Roman orator, philosopher, and statesman Cicero did, that "there is assuredly nothing dearer to a man than wisdom, and though age takes away all else, it undoubtedly brings us that."

And ultimately, we go from "in the way" to "out of the way" and usually then, in front of fellow mourners, we pretend how much we miss those folks we didn't have time for when they walked the earth.

Old and in the way is the modern way that a lot of Americans treat the elderly. They push them to the side. There was a time when the elderly were respected and looked upon for their wisdom and experience. But no more. Some people say that the people who make up the modern world are basically disobedient children—they don't seem to understand that they too someday will be old and in the way.

CHAPTER 56

BLACK MAGIC WOMAN
SANTANA

Originally released on the album *Abraxas*
(Columbia, 1970)
Written by Peter Green

THE BLACK MAGIC WOMAN is the ideal woman—summons demons, holds séances, levitates, is skilled in the art of necromancy, conducts ritualistic orgies with the dead, always out of body, a creature with dark powers and you've got her all to yourself.

Bare breasted, blue veined—short, powerful, and ugly. She provides for you, you're incompetent of doing anything without her—she's the hidden hand, the power behind the throne. Black power, flower power, solar power, you name it—charisma, she's got it. She's what dreams are made of, got the inside track to your consciousness. Puts everybody in your debt, makes others depend on you, she's the bad fairy, the evil genius who turns you into a werewolf, gives you horns and a cloven hoof, but you have no other option.

She's made you wealthy, feared and loaded, put a spoke in your wheel, she's your protector, your guardian. Puts a jinx on your enemies bewitches your competitors, turns your opponents feeble, and any rival that's hostile to you, she makes them weak and flabby, turns them into good losers and fulfills their death wishes.

She's got mesmerizing energy, cuts you off from your vital center, surrounds your inner nature with an adobe wall, and bricks it off with reinforced concrete. She's one in a million, wondrously strange. Stands over you in a military coat, sailor suit—uplifted brassiere, dutch cap and a black snake bullwhip. You're her bellboy, a footman dressed to the nines, double-breasted jacket, evening shirt with a stiff collar, three-pointed pocket hanker-chief. She's witty, literate and well educated. At times you think she's trying to kill you, or maybe she's planning to. Other times you think you might be imagining things.

Her voice gets on your nerves—the low drone, the squeaking sounds, the sing song voice can sound like a cow, a bird, a horse, or the bark of a dog. She's well born, blue blooded, an observer of signs. You consult her on everything especially business transactions, she sees to it that everything goes your way, always at midnight, always on the night before. She feeds on the entrails of your victims, and if you pull back her skin, you'll see the head of an animal.

She's your champion bull-dyke, your spider woman, your hoochie coochie queen, and she puts you on the top level—there's no heights you can't ascend. You're her prototype hero, her straight man, the kingfish, but you're over the hill, on your way to the junk heap, got your hat in your hand—kneeling down, begging her not to abandon you, pleading with her. Aren't you good enough? Why don't you love me? I'll never love you, try and make me.

She's a hard case, full of mumbo jumbo and her kisses have a pungent smell, but you got lucky, you fell into the shithouse and came up with bushels of gold coins. You stepped up the ladder, always a pay raise, you stay in line and you follow the book.

Pug-nosed, grim faced and short on looks—but she's tall and commanding as well. Yellow-blond hair, shoulder length, always barefoot, compassionate eyes, yellow with black pupils, right hand extended outward, palm up.

It's your identity, your psychic field that attracts her. She goes ahead of you or behind you, sometimes falls across your body twisting loosely, for pleasure or pain, for good or ill. Anyone who has a bone to pick with you falls at your feet, she's your tower of strength and you can't let her go. Can't let her slip through your fingers, you'd be lost and ruined, cut off without a cent.

★ ★

LEIGH BRACKETT WAS BORN IN LOS ANGELES

in 1915. She wrote for the science fiction pulps in the early forties but moved to screenplays after Howard Hawks read *No Good from a Corpse*, a detective novel she wrote in 1944. Hawks was looking for a writer who could collaborate with William Faulkner on the Humphrey Bogart movie he was set to direct, an adaptation of Raymond Chandler's novel *The Big Sleep*. Hawks, thinking that Brackett's hard-boiled style would add some blood and guts to the script and unable to glean the author's gender by name alone, famously told his assistant, "Get this Brackett guy." Luckily, that Brackett gal was not offended and helped Faulkner navigate the novel's labyrinthian plot. It was her that Bogart asked who killed Owen Taylor, the chauffeur in the Philip Marlowe story. Brackett, Faulkner, and Hawks were all stumped and a telegram was quickly sent to Chandler, who went back through his book and wired back, "I don't know either."

Brackett soldiered on, discovering that an occasional loose end doesn't detract from a story. She racked up a number of other film credits, including the John Wayne, Dean Martin, Ricky Nelson western *Rio Bravo*, also directed by Howard Hawks. At the time of her death in 1978, she had just completed the first draft of *The Empire Strikes Back*, the second *Star Wars* movie, leaving subsequent drafts to be written by George Lucas and Larry Kasdan.

Leigh Brackett never stopped writing western, crime and science fiction pretty much up until the end. In the June 1949 issue of *Thrilling Wonder Stories* Brackett published a gripping story titled "Sea Kings of Mars," which became one of her best novels under the new title *The Sword of Rhiannon*. Reading this story, one can see why Lucas tapped Brackett for the *Star Wars* sequel. The book travels through time and the solar system yet feels as familiarly exciting as a western serial at a Saturday matinee. Lead character Matt Carse even has a bit of Indiana Jones about him as he searches for a hidden cavern on Mars where the Martian god Rhiannon is said to have been imprisoned by other deities for giving advanced technology, including weaponry, to early races on the red planet millennia ago.

It was in this context that Brackett presaged the third of Arthur C. Clarke's three laws of science fiction—*Any sufficiently advanced technology is indistinguishable from magic*. She wrote, "Witchcraft to the ignorant . . . simple science to the learned," implying that Rhiannon's gift, commonplace in Matt Carse's home era, seemed like magical miracles in the pre-technological past.

Yet one place where additional learning does not disentangle the mystery of the subject is music. As a matter of fact, the argument can be made that the more you study music, the less you understand it. Take two people—one studies contrapuntal music theory, the other cries when they hear a sad song. Which of the two really understands music better?

E. B. White had a saying about humor that seems applicable to music: Analyzing humor is like dissecting a frog. Few people are interested, and the frog dies of it. But that has never stopped people from depending on facts, laws, rules, and structure so much that the joy of discovery is leached out and the magic in the melody is sucked away.

And then there are the lyrics. Often is heard a discouraging word about the work generated from Tin Pan Alley. It became common to dismiss these songs with their moon/June/spoon rhyme schemes and simple structures. And often, when you see them on the page, they seem so slight, it's hard to believe there is a song there at all.

But it's important to remember that these words were written for the ear and not for the eye. And as in comedy, where a seemingly simple sentence can transform into a joke through the magic of performance, an inexplicable thing happens when words are set to music. The miracle is in their union.

In the same way that Velcro was invented after the Swiss engineer George de Mestral returned from a hunting trip and was made curious by the thousands of burrs that were attached to his woolen coat and dogs' fur, music naggingly adheres itself in countless pinpoints of memory and emotion. The myriad of rules governing both the literature of lyrics and the mathematics of melody are mere guidelines and those who slavishly follow them, who can only color inside the lines, run the danger of never transcending craft to create anything truly lasting.

"Black Magic Woman" is a fine example. Is it a blues? Music aficionados will regale you with other influences, footnoting other artists and quotations from other songs. Those stridently schooled in the parochial structure of musicality may point at tempo changes and technical folderol like hammer-ons, transposition between various harmonic modes, and the shift between Hungarian and Latin polyrhythms. But none of that speaks to the heart of the song.

And on the page, the lyrics may not impress. In two of the three six-line verses, one of the lines is repeated four times. In the third, only three times. Yet, married to music, the combination becomes hypnotic, rhapsodic, somehow both mysterious and direct as a telegram. Like a great painting, it has depth, somehow different each time you approach and illuminated from somewhere deep inside, inviting repeated contemplation.

All the self-styled social critics who read lyrics in a deadpan drone to satirize their lack of profundity only show their own limitations. They are as useless as the police officer reading the transcript of Lenny Bruce's act in the courtroom during his obscenity trial. Just as that police officer misses the essential spark in Lenny's performance, so do the others miss the magic that happens when lyrics are wed to music.

Some would call that marriage chemistry, but chemistry seems too based in science and therefore replicable. What happens with words and music is more akin to alchemy, chemistry's wilder, less disciplined precursor, full of experimentation and fraught with failure, with its doomed attempts to turn base metals into gold. People can keep trying to turn music into a science, but in science one and one will always be two. Music, like all art, including the art of romance, tells us time and again that one plus one, in the best circumstances, equals three.

CHAPTER 57

BY THE TIME I GET TO PHOENIX
JIMMY WEBB

Originally released on the album *Ten Easy Pieces*

(Guardian, 1996)

Written by Jimmy Webb

BY THE TIME YOU GET TO PHOENIX IT WILL

be morning where she is, and she'll be just getting out of bed. She raises the shade, walks across the floor, and sees a note that you left on the door. An explanatory message, telling her that you're leaving. She reads the words and no doubt she chuckles, cracks up, the note's got her in stitches, because you've told her this so many times in the past. So many times you left and came back, she knows how your mind shifts, nonstop, and you flip flop about everything, so why would this time be any different, you'll be back. This is not a serious note, and she tosses it in the trash.

By midafternoon you're almost in New Mexico, and you know by this time she'll be working. By day she works nine to five as a massage therapist, hustles clients and answers the call of working stiffs, the rank and file, and she's on active duty. She stops for lunch and gives you a call, you must be back home by now. She calls and lets the phone ring, but there's no answer, it rings and rings and almost vibrates off the wall. Gradually she comes to her senses that there's no one there.

Round about midnight, you're almost in Oklahoma, and you think about now that there's a good chance that she'll be tossing and turning, unable to sleep, going through spasms and calling out your name, delicately and in a lowkey way, almost in a whisper. Then she'll start to cry, weeping and sniveling, shedding tears that slide down her nose and splash on the floor. She wasn't convinced that you'd ever leave her, she never considered it for a minute, but now she knows it's a sure thing. She just never knew that you'd really go.

You tried to tell her a million times, but you couldn't come to grips with it.

You got your money's worth and now you're gone. You didn't even have the courage to kiss her goodbye.

CHAPTER 58

COME ON-A MY HOUSE
ROSEMARY CLOONEY

Originally released as a single

(Columbia, 1951)

Written by Ross Bagdasarian and William Saroyan

THIS IS THE SONG OF SEDUCTION, the big come on. It's calling you to drop in and make the scene, it's out of the way, hush hush. Through the back door, up the back stairs, it's going to give you some tasty fruits, all kinds of things. Fruits and nuts, clusters of grapes with crushed seeds, heaps of pears, and all kinds of leftover pastry, and this song is going to drop it all in your lap. All you have to do is show up.

There's cupboards of crab apples, pink ladies and high breeds, golden apples of the sun. There are pomegranates from the Holy Land, the ones with the thousand seeds, you've got grape seed oil and grape juice, mouthwatering plums with the white wax coating, this song's going to give you everything. Peaches from Persia, everything from the tree of life, pink tinged and dripping with honey, smoked apricots, all the forbidden fruits, and candy, lots of candy.

Gum balls and licorice, jellybeans and snicker bars, this song is going to sucker you in with desserts and multicolored Easter eggs.

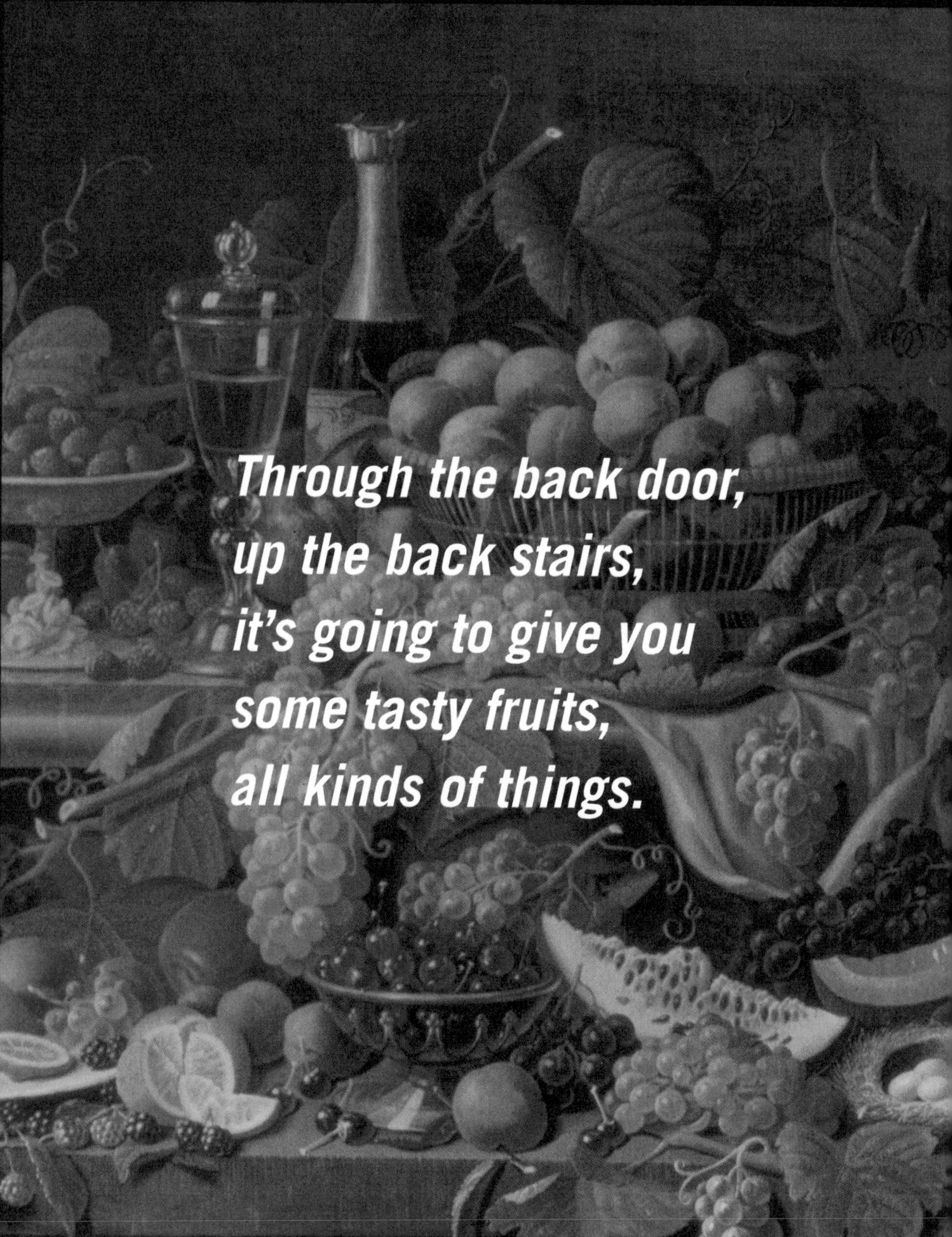

**Through the back door,
up the back stairs,
it's going to give you
some tasty fruits,
all kinds of things.**

It's got a stockpile of dates from fifty million years ago, it's motioning for you to come on in, summoning you, it's got the total universe in there, a whole collection of cakes. Wedding cakes, marble cakes, upside down cakes with frosting, red velvet, strawberry, cheesecake, the works. You're going to get the whole cornucopia, the entire bumper crop. Oodles of apricots, more than enough, the very best. Enough to pig out for a year. Baked peaches and African figs, an oversupply of everything, the whole ball of wax. Even a wedding ring, 24 karat hoop for your finger. You'll even get a Christmas tree, not just a little sapling either, but a full-grown hardwood.

This song is gesturing at you to discover yourself. It's coaxing you, enticing you to come out of retirement and jump in. Are you tempted? You bet. But you're not thinking about what will happen if you're lured in there, you're thinking about what could happen.

★ ★

THIS SONG HAS AN INTERESTING HISTORY.

Clooney was a good pop singer with a jazz sensibility. She knew how to sell a song, even a little trifle like this. It was written by the Pulitzer Prize–winning author William Saroyan and his cousin Ross Bagdasarian as they drove across New Mexico. All the stuff about the exotic fruits and whatnot are part of Armenian hospitality tradition.

Mitch Miller loved novelty records and he gobbled this up, producing the hit version for Ms. Clooney. Too bad he didn't pay more attention to the songwriters. Saroyan didn't do any more songwriting, but his cousin Ross became one of the biggest novelty hitmakers of all time. Under the name David Seville, he sped his voice up and had a bunch of hits as Alvin and the Chipmunks. Ross/David/Alvin can be seen as the piano player who lives across the way from Jimmy Stewart in *Rear Window*.

This is the song of the deviant, the pedophile, the mass murderer. The song of the guy who's got thirty corpses under his basement and human skulls in the refrigerator. This is the kind of song where a black car rolls down the street, a window rolls down and a voice calls out, "Do you want to come over here for a second, little girl? I got some pomegranates for you and figs, dates, and cakes. All kinds of erotic stuff, apples and plums and apricots. Just come on over here for a second." This is a hoodoo song disguised as a happy pop hit. It's a Little Red Riding Hood song. A song sung by a spirit rapper, a warlock.

CHAPTER 59

DON'T TAKE YOUR GUNS TO TOWN

JOHNNY CASH

Originally released as a single
(Columbia, 1958)
Written by Johnny Cash

LIKE IN A ROMANTIC COMEDY, we all know where this song is going from the opening moments. In a romantic comedy, we all know the guy is gonna get the girl, and here, we know things are not gonna go well for Billy.

This is a warning song. Don't be too smart. Always let somebody else think that they are smarter than you. Don't give somebody too many choices. If you have an entire alphabet of letters, just give somebody the A and the B. In this song, a young kid drinks too much whiskey. It's not that he took his guns to town, it's that he got himself drunk and then got shot. Guns and drinking just don't mix. And Johnny Cash knew that as well as anybody. Even as this kid is dying, he remembers what his mother said, but it's too late.

Stories are simple. We all know them. Boy meets girl. Boy loses girl. Boy steals crust of bread. Boy gets gunned down in town square. Girl kills boy's wife. Child grows up searching for father's murderer. Girl marries boy. Boy burns down town.

Taking your guns to town to prove that you are a man might not be the way to go—you might want to rethink things while there is still time left over.

CHAPTER 60

COME RAIN OR COME SHINE
JUDY GARLAND

Originally released on the album *Judy*
(Capitol, 1956)
Music by Howard Arlen
Lyrics by Johnny Mercer

THIS SONG IS A DECLARATION of faith, a solemn vow.

When you love somebody your appreciation is real, you're devoted no matter what. If it rains or it shines, snows or sleets, it doesn't matter, your attachment to each other is bottomless. Whether you're in good humor or dissatisfied it's all the same, and your affection for each other is lodged in the brain, the nervous system. Whether you have peace of mind or you're down in the mouth, this friendship is longstanding and formidable. Upbeat or downbeat, fidelity is beyond question. Your involvement unchanging with wholehearted respect, this love is conclusive and deep in your subconscious.

Your love for each other is diehard and dependable, and it will always be returned, drunk or sober it will be returned. Contented or troubled it will still

be responded to, you can bet on it. Whatever hang-ups and grief might come your way, this love is hardcore. Money or no money it's clear cut and habitual. Throughout all the heartaches and commotion, you're unaffected. You're captivated with each other. You see through each other's eyes, hardly anything gets a rise out of you. You look at things from beginning to end, and you borrow each other's understanding.

★ ★

WHEN THIS SONG WAS FIRST PUBLISHED

in 1946 (for the musical *St. Louis Woman*), it didn't make the charts. But the Harold Arlen (music) and Johnny Mercer (lyrics) composition has generated dozens upon dozens of cover versions spanning a wider range than many standards. Aside from the usual suspects—Frank, Billie, Judy, Ella—you have Don Henley, Bette Midler, James Brown, and many others. Heck, Dr. John recorded it twice.

Perhaps one of the reasons is the earnestness of the lyrics. Earnestness should not be confused with simplicity.

During the sixties, it was popular for self-important scene-makers to belittle so-called Tin Pan Alley hacks with their flower, power, shower, man-of-the-hour rhymes. As is often the case, the facile got lumped in with the truly talented.

Arlen's melody is at once wistful and sure of itself, and Mercer's lyric is matter-of-fact, neither overblown nor containing a shred of irony. And whether it's in service of Judy Garland's razzamatazz "How you like me now?" arrangement or Anita O'Day's cool-kitten reverie over a bed of chamber jazz flutes, the song never seems cloying or false.

It is this very earnestness that most likely led Scorsese to use the song twice in his film *The King of Comedy*. His use of Ray Charles's sweet invocation points out the disconnect in behavior when true obsessiveness masquerades as pure love. Later, when Sandra Bernhard sings the song for a trussed-up Jerry Lewis, there is no mistaking the horrible honesty of her emotion. There is nothing scarier than someone earnest in a delusion.

This song was a big influence on Phil Spector, who took the third line, "High as a mountain and deep as a river," and made it into a musical extravaganza for Tina Turner. He called it "River Deep—Mountain High." Also, around the same time, he had the Turtles, a West Coast pop phenomenon, cop another couple of lines from the second verse of this song in their hit "Happy Together."

CHAPTER 61

DON'T LET ME BE MISUNDERSTOOD
NINA SIMONE

Originally released on the album *Broadway—Blues—Ballads*
(Philips, 1964)
Written by Bennie Benjamin, Horace Ott, and Sol Marcus

THE SONG OF THE BOY WONDER, THE PRODIGY.

The man who knows his stuff, whose cause is honorable and sexually innocent. Whose lust and appetite are as plain as can be, plain as the nose on his face. This is a song of crossed wires and false ideas. Being misquoted and things being taken out of context—things lost in translation, people getting a wrong impression of what you're about.

You're Adam's offspring, a jolly good fellow, a member of the human race, and whatever you do you have it all worked out beforehand, and you're manly and upright about everything, but you go into a rage when your words are perverted or distorted, it can be a real downer. You try to keep a tight leash on yourself and hold yourself back, but you can only go so far, you can't always be a saint, an angel of love—a Michael, a Raphael, or even a Gabriel.

This is a song of crossed wires and false ideas. Being misquoted and things being taken out of context—things lost in translation, people getting a wrong impression of what you're about.

You can't always be a nice guy. Nevertheless, your ulterior motives are always rock solid and sound as a dollar.

Most of the time, you're well liked, lighthearted, and perky—you radiate cheer, bodily pleasure exuberance and bliss, and it's impossible to cover that up. At the same time, you're at your wit's end, embarrassed about everything, puzzled about everything, baffled with your foot in your mouth, and you know that anyone can spot it, that your true colors are recognized and observed, easily detected. All things considered your guiding principles are the very best. You're a gentleman and a scholar and your words are not to be misinterpreted, it makes you argumentative and bitter, a real ugly customer—totally mindless, and it annoys you that someone would take what you say the wrong way or assume anything.

What you're saying is that life has its headaches, its inconveniences, it can be a sea of troubles and that you've had your equal portion of all of it. As things stand you just don't want your words to be misread or twisted around. You don't want to be taken for granted, above all by someone you love. You want to keep everything within bounds, your affection on the highest level. Completely genuine from head to toe. But you're only an earthling, a John Doe, a man in the street and you have opinions and assumptions that are dear, sometimes they prick your heart, backfire, make you hate yourself.

Being misunderstood can get on your nerves. Some cockeyed thing, some asinine thing, some common garden variety thing, and it beats you down, makes you feel underappreciated.

The thing about being misunderstood is that it diminishes your enjoyment of life.

★ ★

MOTHER DIED TODAY.

Or did she?

When Gilbert Stuart first translated Albert Camus's 1942 French novel *The Stranger* into English, that first sentence seemed straightforward enough. But it has generated verbiage many times the word count of the book itself, as translators have gotten themselves mired in not only the ambiguities and time paradoxes of French verb tenses that don't exist in English, but also how the order of words in sentences weights those tenses.

And then there is the matter of Mother herself. In the original French of the opening line: "*Aujourd'hui, maman est morte,*" Camus uses *maman* purposely instead of *mère*, which is the more formal word for mother. *Maman* is more colloquial, somewhere between Mommy and Mum, so from the beginning, the translator miscolors the narrator's relationship with his dead parent.

Subsequent translators and commentators have parsed the language, trying to pull themselves up from the morass of varied French verb tenses—to explain the difference between *passé simple* and *passé composé.* It is not easy. From the 1700s to the late 1900s there was even an informal rule to help French authors choose between the two tenses. Called the Twenty-Four-Hour Rule, introduced by the French printer and scholar Henri Estienne, it stated that the *passé composé* had to be used for events taking place within a single twenty-four-hour period, but anything outside that period could use the *passé simple.*

And then you have to realize this is only one problem arising from one sentence in one book in one language and you start to understand just what L. L. Zamenhof was thinking. Zamenhof was a Polish ophthalmologist who thought barriers between languages created walls that stopped the flow of ideas, impeding friendships and alliances between cultures and countries.

Realizing the difficulty in learning a single foreign language, Zamenhof created Esperanto in the late 1800s in the hopes that it might become a

"universal second language," a simplified tongue everyone could learn without sacrificing their native dialect. That way, local vernacular could thrive and you would be able to communicate with anyone in the world.

There are many reasons why it failed. Fascists gained strength from keeping people separated and ill-informed, and they denounced the international language. Nazis and Stalinists publicly decried Zamenhof's dream. And then there were those who thought Esperanto speakers were flaunting God's word and, by learning to speak in one common tongue, were threatening to build another Tower of Babel.

Today, Esperanto is still around, though some remember it best as the inspiration for ESP-Disk, a New York–based record label formed in 1963 with the objective of releasing Esperanto-based music, but today remembered for recordings by Albert Ayler, Pharoah Sanders, William Burroughs, and the Fugs. And you can use Google to translate to and from Esperanto.

But language isn't the only bar to understanding each other—there is inflection and implication. When burglar Derek Bentley said to his accomplice Christopher Craig, "Let him have it, Chris," he was charged as party to the crime of murder when Craig shot the London policeman trying to stop them. In his defense, Bentley said what he meant by his line was let him have the gun.

He didn't need a translator to be misunderstood.

In 1964 Horace Ott had a fight with his girlfriend and teamed up with fellow songwriters Bennie Benjamin and Sol Marcus. They wrote "Don't Let Me Be Misunderstood" and gave it to Nina Simone.

She brought her own artistry to it and nowadays the static between Horace Ott and his unnamed girlfriend is long forgotten. The song can be sung by anyone who feels they are not getting through to a loved one. But the song has taken on more meanings as Nina's measured, defiant delivery has been adopted by some as an understated social equality anthem.

Songs can do that. Like any other piece of art, songs are not seeking to be understood. Art can be appreciated or interpreted but there is seldom anything to understand. Whether it's *Dogs Playing Poker* or *Mona Lisa*'s smile, you gain nothing from understanding it.

Perhaps you can gain something by understanding the context behind a painting like *The Raft of the Medusa* by Théodore Géricault or be titillated by the torn-from-today's-headlines energy of Banksy's latest broadside, but in either case there is room for your feelings, your opinion.

Sometimes art can be a blunt fist—the colored rectangles of Mark Rothko, the copious polka dots of Yayoi Kusama, or John Lennon's inexhaustible repetition of the phrase "I want you" in a single song. These are artists so in control of their tools that they know exactly what they are doing. Yet some people in their rush to judge brand the work simplistic.

Don't let me be misunderstood.

CHAPTER 62

STRANGERS IN THE NIGHT
FRANK SINATRA

Originally released as a single
(Reprise, 1966)
Music by Bert Kaempfert
Lyrics by Charles Singleton and Eddie Snyder

THE SONG OF THE LONE WOLF, THE OUTSIDER,

the alien, the foreigner, and night owl who's wheeling and dealing, putting everything up for sale and surrendering his self-interest. On the move aimlessly through the dingy darkness—slicing up the pie of sentimental feelings, dividing it into pieces all the time, exchanging piercing penetrating looks with someone he hardly knows.

Tramps and mavericks, the object of each other's affection, enraptured with each other and creating an alliance—ignoring all the ages of man, the golden age, electronic age, age of anxiety, the jazz age. You're here to tell a different story, a bird of another feather. You've got a tough persona, like a side of beef, and you're aroused and stimulated, with an ear-to-ear grin, like a Cheshire cat, and you're rethinking your entire formless life, your entire being is filled with a whiff of this heady ambrosia. Something in your vital spirit, your pulse, something that runs in the blood, tells you that you must have this tender feeling of love now and forever, this essence of devoted love held tightly in your grip—that it's essential and necessary for staying alive and cheating death.

Intruders, oddballs, kooks, and villains, in this gloomy lifeless dark, fight for space. Two rootless alienated people, withdrawn and isolated, opened the door to each other, said Aloha, Howdy, How you doing, and Good Evening. How could you have known that the smooching and petting, eros and adoration was just one break down mambo hustle away—one far sided google eyed look and a lusty leer—that ever since then, that moment of truth, you've been steamed up, head over heels, each other's hearts' desire. Sweethearts and honeys right from the beginning. Right from the inaugural sidelong sneak peek, the origin—the starting point. Now you're yoked together, one flesh in perpetuity—into the vast eternity—immortalized.

★ ★

BY THE TIME FRANK SINATRA STEPPED INTO

the studio to record "Strangers in the Night" on April 11, 1966, he had already been singing professionally for thirty-one years and recording since 1939. He had seen trends come and go in popular music and had, in fact, set trends himself and spawned scores of imitators for decades.

Still, it was amazing that the soundtrack of the summer of 1966, according to the July 2 edition of the *Billboard* Hot 100, was topped by that little pop song. Amazingly, in the middle of the British Invasion, "Strangers in the Night" by Hoboken's own beat out the Beatles' "Paperback Writer" and the Rolling Stones' "Paint It Black." Today, the charts are so stratified and niche marketed, you would never see something like this happen. Nowadays, everyone stays in their own lane, guaranteeing themselves top honors in their own category even if that category is something like Top Klezmer Vocal Performance on a Heavy Metal Soundtrack Including Americana Samples.

But Frank had to slug it out with everybody, even though "Strangers" was a song he hated, one that he regularly dismissed as "a piece of shit." But let us not forget, Howlin' Wolf allegedly once said the same thing about his first electric guitar and the Chess brothers put that quote in big letters on one of his album covers.

Frank may have hated the song, but the fact of the matter is, he chose it. And therein lies a tale. By the time we had heard "Strangers in the Night," it had gone through at least two sets of lyrics and a few people had already laid claim to its authorship. It's a confusing tale that spans a couple of continents. I present it here in the interests of entertainment and will not swear to its veracity.

Many cigar smokers have enjoyed the Avo XO, a fine Dominican cigar. The well-known Swiss tobacconist Davidoff of Geneva introduced them to the world and now more than two million a year are sold. These cigars were a rebound revenue stream for an Armenian musician, a Beiruti immigrant living in New York, who felt he had been swindled out of the profits of a chart-topping composition.

As a youth, Avo Uvezian was a jazz pianist, playing his way across the Middle East during the early forties, at one point teaching Iran's Shah Reza Pahlavi how to correctly swing-dance. With the grateful shah's help, Uvezian relocated to New York in 1947 and enrolled at the Juilliard School of Music.

Here is where the story gets murky. According to Uvezian, he sent one of the little melodies he composed to the only person he knew in the music industry—the German orchestra leader and composer Bert Kaempfert. Today that melody, under the title "Strangers in the Night," is listed as a Bert Kaempfert composition.

One way or another, the song was presented to Frank Sinatra. According to legend, Frank requested the lyrics be changed. Charles Singleton and Eddie Snyder were brought in. They took the melancholy song about parting lovers titled "Broken Guitar" and returned a week later with "Strangers in the Night." Interestingly, Charles Singleton also co-wrote "Tryin' to Get to You," a song recorded in 1954 by Washington, DC, vocal group the Eagles. That song was again recorded the following year by Elvis Presley while he was on Sun Records.

Other people also made claims against Bert Kaempfert's authorship of "Strangers in the Night." One was made by the Croatian singer Ivo Robić and another by the French composer Philippe-Gérard, though neither has held up as well as Avo Uvezian's.

And as for him, his name is not on the record label, but it is on a lot of cigar bands. He maintained a good attitude and lived joyfully into his nineties. Though he shrugged off the music business, he did not shrug off music, performing regularly and entertaining friends with his piano playing while enjoying millions of dollars of Swiss cigar money. Not all stories have to have sad endings.

And as far as I know, no one has ever contested the writing of Frank's hit from the following year, "Somethin' Stupid," though it is worth mentioning that it was written by Van Dyke Parks's older brother Carson.

CHAPTER 63

VIVA LAS VEGAS
ELVIS PRESLEY

Originally released as a single

(RCA, 1964)

Written by Doc Pomus and Mort Shuman

THE SONG OF THE GAMBLER, the sportsman—luck of the draw—short odds, long odds, a flip of the coin, raffles, lottos and the devil's bones. The roulette wheel, pinball machine, the switched-on city, the star-spangled city. This is the place where your personality bursts into flame. This is the place you take calculated risks, where you defy danger and run up a fortune, like Rothschild, Hobbs, DuPont, Vanderbilt—spending money like water, like a drunken sailor. Boomtown of all boomtowns. Living beyond your means, a blinding sort of place. You put up the money and you boost up the odds. Money mongering, living on credit, telling everybody you're able to pay. Long live this place, with its ever so many countless women—the broads and dames, chicks and dolls, escorts, partners, and bodyguards. All the women folk, wide open, free living—dancing on the razor's edge.

You don't stop even for a second, not even for a breath. You're the sharpie, the demon worshipper, the boogie man with extra lust. Long live this place.

You never take a break and you never hit the sack. No time to loaf and lounge around, you're going full blast. If only there were eighty more hours in the day. Crap shooting, card cutting, casting lots and coin matching, head calling, keno and bingo. You're coming into money and you're dropping into a good thing. You shuffle the cards and bottom out. Six figure income thrown in the gutter, losing a king's ransom, and winning a gold mine. You've got an atomic powered inner spirit, sturdy as an ox—made of iron and tough as naked steel. Nerves that are ramrod stiff, and hard as marble.

Las Vegas, crossroads of the modern world. Utopia, Garden of Eden, Land of Dreams. If you see it once, even with half an eye you're never the same. All it takes is just one glance, and you're transformed, mutated into something else, some arcane substance with a perpetual smile—something rich and strange. You keep the pot boiling, strutting, and strolling, stretching your legs, jaywalking, and making the scene. You're quick on the trigger like grease lightning. Shaking like jelly with plenty of verve and gusto. Chirping like a cricket and spreading cheer—having a blast in the gambling hell. You're singing the praises of the city you love. The city that turns morning into midnight, and midnight into morning, changes after hours into early dawn. The close of the day becomes the first flash of blinding light—invisible radiation, blinking and twinkling, gleaming and dazzling—busting the light meter. It costs you your last dime, and you suffer losses, and dribble away your last dollar. You're all used up and you end up like a pauper, washed up and wrinkled like a prune—dealt a knockout blow. You're going for broke this time, going full speed, jazzed up and asking the Fortune Lady to heat the dice, make sure the ball bounces your way—that the law of averages is on your side. You want to shoot the works, hit the bull's eye, and beat the system. You want to come out on top of the heap, and you don't want it to be over too soon.

★ ★

THIS IS A SONG ABOUT FAITH. The kind of faith where

you step under a shower spigot in the middle of a desert and fully believe water will come out. Or, more to the point, the type of faith where you stand in the marble lobby of an opulent hotel with neon flashin' while being served free drinks by a thousand pretty women wearing sequined leotards flirting for tips in a bright-light city full of pawnshops and suicides and you still think you're going to win. No wonder it sets your soul on fire.

"Viva Las Vegas" is also a commercial. Of course, when Elvis first recorded this Doc Pomus–Mort Shuman composition in 1963 and released it in 1964, he didn't know that five years later, in July of 1969, the subject of this bright and breezy love song would become the hub of his live performances—and that in turn, the famed man-made nocturnal oasis would vampirically indulge his worst habits and impulses.

Among a certain cadre of fans, Colonel Tom Parker is equally reviled for squandering Elvis's talents in increasingly substandard movies and holding him in stasis in Las Vegas by allowing the Hilton a sweetheart deal to help off-set the manager's staggering gambling debt. Famously, Elvis's health and performance spiraled downward but still, he was paraded out night after night. The spectacle began to resemble something out of P. T. Barnum, who would promote a star attraction well past their prime as a curiosity just to get people into the tent. In this case Elvis was that curiosity and the tent was Vegas, and if people were ultimately disappointed by the star's dissolution there were plenty of other distractions to take their minds off it. And to take their money. All lessons the Colonel learned somewhere between the Netherlands of his birth and the carnivals where he was truly born.

Someone once told me about a faith healer who had clean-cut confederates standing at the doors of his revival meetings to offer a complimentary wheelchair to anyone who had difficulty walking—anyone on crutches, with a cane, a walker, or even a pronounced limp. They were told there was a wheelchair

section near the side of the stage. The faith healer would come out and recognize his chairs and have one of those people brought onstage. He tells the crowd that person doesn't need the wheelchair. In fact, he already knows it. He tells the person to get up and walk. When that person does, the people cheer, believing they've seen a miracle, not knowing that person was already walking in under their own power. That's the way the hustle works.

But the interesting thing is, you talk to the guy in the wheelchair, and he believes it too. It's powerful medicine to be onstage and have people cheering for you. Adrenaline, endorphins, and who knows what else were pumping through that person's system and he probably actually was without pain for the first time in maybe his whole life. No matter how you explain to him what just happened, he too thinks he was part of a miracle. And that's how faith works. And real hustles, the really good ones, have to have a little faith in them. Like W. C. Fields said: "You can't cheat an honest man."

In the Elvis myth, it's easy to paint the Colonel as Judas tossing silver into the one-armed bandits thirty pieces at a time, but it's important to remember that there would have been no King to be brought low without the Colonel's hard work and unwavering faith from the beginning. And even in the darkest hours, the Colonel was loyal and true, worshipping no pretenders to the throne, no false gods, no other clients. Even after Elvis's death, the Colonel stayed at the Hilton to make sure that all tributes were kept respectful, though cynics often pointed out that the Colonel allowed himself to become a tourist attraction to continue paying off his own steadily increasing gambling markers.

Meanwhile song co-writer Doc Pomus, though also wheelchair-bound, didn't need any faith healing—he held his faith somewhere between four of a kind and a straight flush. Finding songwriting too chancy, he quit for the relative security of dealing high-stakes poker games out of his Manhattan apartment, quitting that only when one of the players left the table one night and washed up in the East River. Soon after that, B.B. King and Dr. John knocked on Doc's door and dragged him back to the merely metaphorically cutthroat world of music.

Today, Elvis is gone, the Colonel is gone, Doc Pomus is gone. B.B. and Dr. John are gone. Meanwhile Hilton now owns thirty-one hotels in Las Vegas.

The house always wins.

Viva Las Vegas.

CHAPTER 64

SATURDAY NIGHT AT THE MOVIES THE DRIFTERS

Originally released as a single
(Atlantic, 1964)
Written by Barry Mann and Cynthia Weil

SAVVY OBSERVERS HAD A CLUE that the music industry was in trouble when one of the most popular genres was dubbed "alternative." This is patently impossible since, by definition, alternative is a challenge to the conventional norm—that is, a different choice from the most popular.

Modern filmmakers find themselves in a similar quandary. That doesn't mean they aren't making interesting, thought-provoking movies. It just means the counterculture has superseded mainstream culture. Trying to figure out where we stand as an audience can make us feel like Paul Newman in *Cool Hand Luke* when Strother Martin tells him, "What we have here is a failure to communicate."

In the seventies, antiheroes like Butch and Sundance, Dirty Harry, Super Fly, and Travis Bickle thumbed their noses at fifty years of ramrod-straight backbones and firm jaws. Saturday night at the movies had always been more than just a chance to share a bucket of popcorn with a date in the last row of the balcony. The best features contained wisdom, aphorisms that hinted at a moral code, a code that could reach its audience more easily than the sermons that served it up with a helping of hellfire fearmongering each Sunday morn.

Not that there weren't antiheroes before the seventies, like the aforementioned Wild One, Jimmy Cagney and Edward G. Robinson in the early thirties gangster movies, or James Dean in *Rebel Without a Cause*. But those characters either paid for their deviance, or they were defanged and returned to the straight and narrow by the end of the final reel.

Similarly, just as alternative became the only alternative, the antihero crowded real heroes off the screen until anyone who even hinted at Gene Autry's cowboy code was banished and branded obsolete. Meanwhile any film that had the audacity to offer any kind of message, either uplifting or merely thought-provoking, was politicized by one side of the audience or the other and championed only by its predetermined constituency. There was so much preaching to the choir that they may as well have just shown the movies on Sunday morning as Saturday night.

Sequels and remakes roll off the assembly line nowadays with alarming frequency and astronomical budgets but they still can't recapture the wonder and magic of the originals. They fail to transport us from our seats in the balcony to a world of wonder. Hell, for the most part, they can't even convince people to get out of their living rooms to see the damn thing.

People will tell you they don't watch old movies for a bunch of reasons—because they are in black and white or maybe there's a two-minute sequence that changing times have rendered politically incorrect. These people lack imagination and are fine throwing out the baby with the bathwater.

Those who dismiss movies from before their time as merely simplistic are missing out on Kirk Douglas's bravura performance in Billy Wilder's *Ace in the Hole*, which predicted the toxicity of media manipulation, and Brando in

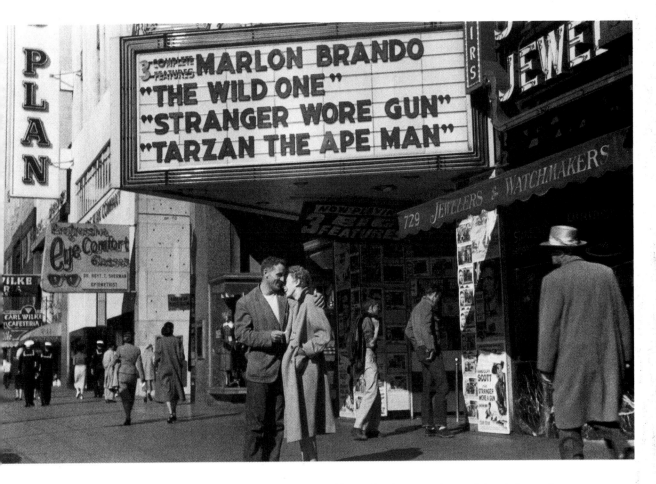

On the Waterfront as dockworker Terry Malloy, who learns it's not his night and testifies against a corrupt union boss who had his brother killed. The movie is so strong, you don't even need the historical context of Elia Kazan and the HUAC hearings for it to hit you in the guts.

High Noon is far from a mere western. It's a nuanced tale of a man facing down the clock, learning about bravery, loyalty, faith, and love. It's been re-made in the big city as well as with mobsters and even with Sean Connery as an off-world federal agent who gets on the wrong side of a hit man at a mining colony on one of Jupiter's moons.

A character study like *The Heiress* allowed Olivia de Havilland to bring a more complex type of female character to the screen, while *Sweet Bird of Youth* pushed the boundaries of acceptability even when the Tennessee Williams stage play was cleaned up for the neighborhood movie house. The tension in both of these films came partially from pushing at those walls, from not being allowed to say everything. Having to infer always makes you choose more carefully.

Then there's *The Treasure of the Sierra Madre*. It stands up to this day as pure entertainment but carries with it the deeper themes of avarice and paranoia, corruption, and the increasingly harmful effects of desolation.

It was a hard shoot and Jack Warner was at wit's end when the filming of the B. Traven novel about the search for gold in the Sierra Madre mountains ran astronomically over budget. But in the end it was worth it, earning three Academy Awards, including one for Walter Huston, who acted in the film, and another for his son, John, who directed it. Everyone knows that young Robert

Blake appears as the newsboy but fewer people know that the mysterious author of the novel, B. Traven, supposedly appears as an extra in the flophouse scene.

And we can't forget *12 Angry Men*. Lock strong actors in a room with a well-written, compelling story. It seems simple but it's so seldom done. Sidney Lumet directed what might be the first indie movie ever made, costing maybe three hundred thousand dollars. Most of the budget went to the powerhouse cast, who spend an hour and a half showing that it only takes one person to be a hero and how every story has many shades of gray even when it's filmed in black and white. Maybe especially when it's filmed in black and white. This movie has been satirized, lampooned, rewritten, imitated, reimagined, remade, and modernized. But never improved upon.

America has always been a great melting pot but there are a few things that have been created here and then given back to the world. As much fun as it is to drive a Ferrari, Detroit will always be the automobile's home. As good a player as Stéphane Grappelli is, you have to go back to King Oliver, Buddy Bolden, and Louis Armstrong to find the beating heart of jazz. Likewise, Fellini, Kurosawa, and their counterparts around the world have made some terrific movies but we all know where the film industry got its first slap on the ass and drew its initial breath.

People keep talking about making America great again. Maybe they should start with the movies.

STEREO
CS 9505

CL 2705

COLUMBIA

STEREO
"360 SOUND"

Pete
Seeger
Waist
Deep
in
The Big
Muddy
and
Other
Love
Songs

CHAPTER 65

WAIST DEEP IN THE BIG MUDDY PETE SEEGER

Originally released on the album
Waist Deep in the Big Muddy and Other Love Songs
(Columbia, 1967)
Written by Pete Seeger

THIS SONG IS A REMEMBRANCE OF THINGS

past, you're looking back to olden times, to things that have happened before now. You're in a militia, a volunteer army. A newcomer, a raw recruit, practicing tactics and playing war games in the swamplands. You're learning how to take fire, trigger mines and throw bombs.

In the dark of night, the Skipper tells you to cut across a tributary stream, the big muddy, and you're knee-deep in it. The platoon leader says to push on, but a noncommissioned officer questions that. He says to the chief—are you confident that this is the best way to get back to the terminal. The way things are stacking up it doesn't look too good. The chief will have none of it, says I've crossed this river a mile up before, and these questions are unwarranted.

It might get a little spongy but just keep slogging, keep advancing, we'll be on terra firma in no time.

Before you know it, you're waist deep in the muck, and you're starting to get concerned. Still though the head honcho says continue on, keep moving, no ifs ands or buts. The sergeant says—Sir we're too loaded down with baggage and contraptions, we'll be dragged under. The commander says—Don't be silly your arguments are baseless, come on man show some backbone and will-power, do like me, come on let's get this show on the road. But now you're neck deep in the slush, and still the wacko captain says to keep going. Pretty soon there's a murky dark shadow over your head, and you hear a splashing and gurgling, the top dog's helmet comes floating by, the Sergeant says—turn around men and go back, I'm the big gun now, do as I say.

You plunge into the slimy deep, descend down to the bottom, and you see your dead leader's body stuck in the muddy quagmire. He didn't know that the water was deeper here than the place he was before, didn't realize he was walking towards the drop-off. Hadn't known that a second stream was lumped together with this one and that the cross current would swirl around and pull him down. You narrowly escaped from the big muddy, but the old war horse is long gone.

It was by accident that you got out of there, you had a lucky break, the nutty captain wasn't so lucky, and the unfortunate incident nauseated you, but you're not going to come down on anybody, or implicate anybody, you just want to wash your hands and be free of it. When you see the standard reports in the news of this tragic event, that old feeling can't help but come back. That we are always deep in a gigantic, colossal mess, and some big idiot is telling us to push on. It would take a lifetime to relive all your memories. You want to do it all in a day.

★ ★

QUITE OFTEN THERE IS THE WHIFF OF THE

killjoy in the exposure of subterfuge. Whether it be the proud know-it-all refocusing misdirected attention on a gimmicked coin at a magic show, or a local TV reporter exposing some kind of modern medical quackery, there's no mistaking the smug smile as they remind their audience that they were one up on them.

However, the illumination of facts surrounding the oft-repeated belief that lemmings follow each other off cliffs in mass ritualistic suicide is not meant to disillusion nor disappoint. On the contrary, this story of Rodentia hari-kari is chock-full of entertaining lies and chicanery. It is enjoyable in the same way a flask of whiskey can be on a cold winter night, fine to savor alone, better when shared.

The image of lemmings rushing en masse to their shared doom has become such a common and vivid image that it's hard to believe that it has only solidified as animal legend since the late 1950s as a falsified part of an Academy Award–winning documentary from the Walt Disney Company.

Between 1955 and 1958 James R. Simon was one of nine photographers Disney sent to produce the documentary *White Wilderness*, a breathtaking full-color close-up look at animal life in the savage and cruel environment of the North American Arctic. After assignments were divvied up, Simon was tasked with documenting the behavior of the lemming—a small rounded rodent, cousin to the common rat and gerbil, with a flat claw on each front paw to help dig in the snowy areas they call home.

Sometimes the difference between religion and science can be measured in the distance between the unanswered and the unanswerable question. People live in fear. For instance, at the end of the day when the sun disappeared people were afraid it might never come back. Religion calmed them with a solution to the unanswerable question—the Greek god Helios dragged the sun across the sky every morning in a golden chariot. It was his job, he would do it every day, and that calmed the fear of living in darkness.

Time passed and science made discoveries and unanswerable questions began to get answered. The Earth spun on its axis and revolved around the sun. Helios retired.

Migration habits were really mysterious because they happened across such large areas and over time as well. No one knew where birds went in the winter. People used to believe they slept like bears in underground caves. Then we learned different.

Lemmings migrate to more spacious areas when their population density becomes overwhelming. Because they are traveling through terrain unknown to them, there is a certain number of casualties and it's not unusual to find their small bodies at the foot of cliffs or drowned in unfamiliar lakes and rivers in their quest for new open space. But it's not mass suicide, though locals and hunters did tell tales.

Enter James Simon and the Disney film crew. The truth was not very photogenic, and Simon was already well versed in the difficulties nature documentarians faced in getting their subjects to perform on cue. Simon used a number of film tricks to build a dramatic sequence. He bought a dozen lemmings and shot them from a number of angles to multiply their numbers. He placed them on a crowded turntable to give the illusion of migratory freneticism and then, finally, chased them off of a cliff himself into the Bow River below, making it look like a surge of mob mentality had driven them mad and ultimately to their watery grave.

The image of these small creatures blindly following each other to their doom also became a common metaphor for mindless groups, like the obedient platoon in the Pete Seeger song who followed their stubborn commanding officer into the Mississippi River near a Louisiana training camp until he was swallowed up by quicksand. Luckily, a quick-thinking sergeant turned them around and marched them back to base.

That song, "Waist Deep in the Big Muddy," is totally true. Perhaps.

Pete Seeger, along with the rest of the Weavers, had been banned from television in the early fifties. It was the McCarthy era and Pete's left-leaning politics and refusal to testify or sign papers for the House Un-American Activities Committee had kept him off of television well into the following decade. But it didn't stop him from singing and playing and spreading messages both political and cultural in more intimate live settings.

Come 1967, Tom and Dick Smothers broke the seventeen-year ban by inviting Pete onto their CBS program. Pete performed a number of songs, among them one he had recently written, "Waist Deep in the Big Muddy." When William Paley heard the song at rehearsal and realized the lyrics were Pete's allegory of the quagmire escalating in Vietnam, Paley cut the song from the show. The CBS boss didn't want a repeat of a recent experience where he had been woken at three in the morning by an angry LBJ after a sketch lampooning him ran on the same program.

Needless to say, the brothers were furious. But a year later, momentum shifted. Even Walter Cronkite broke his usual stance of neutrality and spoke against the war. Pete Seeger returned to CBS and sang "Big Muddy" for the *Smothers Brothers* audience. It made news when he didn't sing it and it made news when he did.

That's because everybody was tuned in to the same TV shows—people against the war, people in favor of it. We all had a shared baseline cultural vocabulary. People who wanted to see the Beatles on a variety show had to watch flamenco dancers, baggy-pants comics, ventriloquists, and maybe a scene from Shakespeare. Today, the medium contains multitudes and man needs only pick one thing he likes and feast exclusively on a stream dedicated to it.

There's twenty-four hours of blues, surf music, left-wing whining, right-wing badgering, any stripe of belief imaginable. There are stories as interesting as lemming suicides and totally true, like the fact that whale songs have inexplicably lowered in pitch 30 percent since the sixties. But these stories are buried on animal documentary channels, where they will probably never capture the general public's imagination.

Turns out, the best way to shut people up isn't to take away their forum—it's to give them all their own separate pulpits. Ultimately most folks will listen to what they already know and read what they already agree with. They will devour pale retreads of the familiar and perhaps never get to discover they might have a taste for Shakespeare or flamenco dancing. It's the equivalent of letting an eight-year-old pick their own diet. Inevitably they'll choose chocolate for every meal and end up undernourished with rotted teeth and weighing five hundred pounds.

Somewhere between Pete's "big fool" and lemmings being chased off a cliff.

CHAPTER 66

WHERE OR WHEN
DION

Originally released on the album *Presenting Dion and the Belmonts*
(Laurie, 1959)
Music by Richard Rodgers
Lyrics by Lorenz Hart

THIS IS A SONG OF REINCARNATION, one repetitious drone through space, plugging the same old theme, nonstop over and over again, where every waking moment bears a striking resemblance to something that happened in pre-Revolutionary times, pre-Renaissance times or pre-Christian times, where everything is exactly alike, and you can't tell anything apart. History keeps repeating itself, and every moment of life is the same moment, with more than one level of meaning.

You were having a discourse, rambling on, thinking out loud, discussing things—letting your hair down, having eyeball to eyeball encounters, playing peekaboo—going backwards, forwards, to and fro—without any difference, with an inkling that it all happened earlier, but you can't pinpoint the location the district or the region, and now it's happening again, one timeless moment identical to the next—full of memory lapses and mental blocks, it's an

Where the past has a way of showing up in front of you and coming into your life without being called.

otherworldly feeling, built on air but down to earth, like a pipe dream—like a visual lifetime image that's here to stay.

The outfits, garments, hoods, the Sunday finery, the fur-lined coats, things that were worn back in the day, back in the days of antiquity, are exactly the same. The apron, the robe, the brassiere, the rayon stockings, and waist belt, just like in ancient times—never out of date. Stitches, buttonholes, knitting and embroidery, putting on the dog—ragged out—zoot suit, windbreaker, flannel pants, suede gloves and undershirt—wooden shoes—all decked out and fit to kill. Not a bit of difference between that occasion and this one—six of one, half a dozen of the other. A dead ringer for the actual thing, unchanged and consistent from the year One. Right from when the curtain first rose, the same regalia, same mustachio, toupee, same phenomenal world appearing and reappearing, telling, and retelling. Same old song, same old tune, same riddles—fighting the same old battle all in the same breath, and you can be absolutely sure that it happened before and will happen again—it's inevitable.

The handshake, the glad hand, the same coincidence time after time. The kissing, embracing, breaking apart and coming together, being roguish and playful, teasing, slapping and hitting—busting a gut—putting each other in stitches, yukking it up and rejoicing good naturedly. Getting high on each other, getting a load of each other, adoring each other—to each other we'll be true, to each other we're just what the doctor ordered. The profanity, the shallowness, being born—reborn and born again the regeneration of it all. That's the ultimate aim.

Life in the wasteland, where there's no tomorrow and it always seems like only yesterday, where we share the same faults over and over, where reincarnation overtakes you. Where the past has a way of showing up in front of you and coming into your life without being called.

Where if it's not happening now, it wasn't happening then or ever.

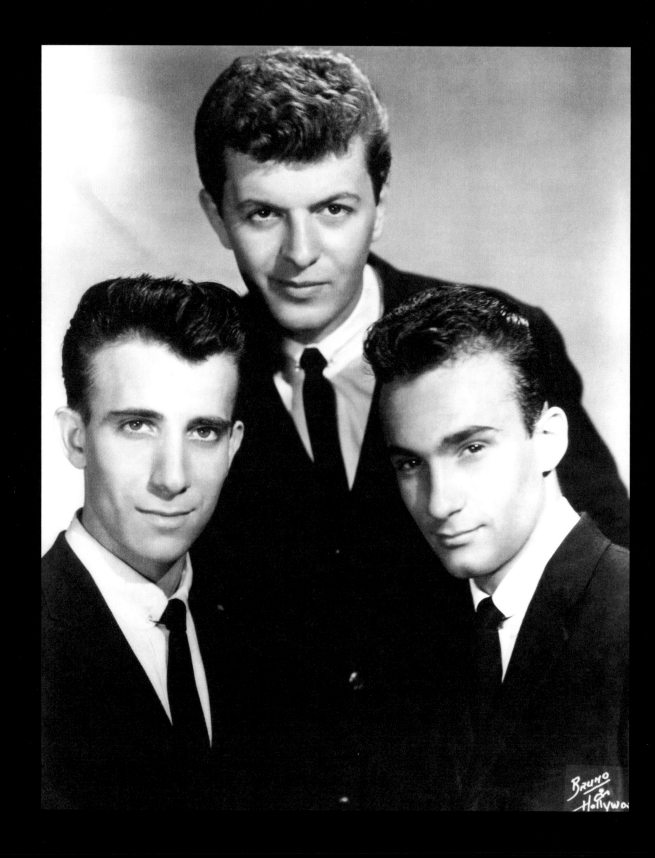

★ ★

I FEEL LIKE I'VE ALREADY WRITTEN ABOUT

this song before. But that's understandable because "Where or When" dances around the outskirts of our memory, drawing us in with images of the familiar being repeated and beguiling us with lives not yet lived.

Debuting in the 1937 Broadway show *Babes in Arms*, the song pairs Lorenz Hart lyrics with music by Richard Rodgers. Many famous Rodgers and Hart songs were also in the score of that play, including "The Lady Is a Tramp," "Johnny One Note," and "My Funny Valentine."

Contrary to what you might think, that last song is not a paean to some unnamed object of desire. It's actually sung by the character Billie Smith to the eponymous Valentine LaMar delineating some of his shortcomings, mouth weak and sad physique, before revealing that ultimately the smile he brings to her heart is enough to bring her happiness.

Two years after its stage debut, the film version of *Babes in Arms* was made. But the Busby Berkeley–directed film, uniting Mickey Rooney and Judy Garland, was barely recognizable, cut down to a simplified husk as Hollywood was afraid of the original's political overtones.

The more unusual characters in the play, among them a Nietzsche-spouting communist and a Southern racist, were excised from the show. Also, somehow, many of the most famous Rodgers and Hart collaborations were also lost in the transition.

But one song remained from draft to draft and indeed drifts from the stage to the screen like a half-grasped recollection. That song, of course, is "Where or When."

"Some things that happened for the first time seem to be happening again."

By the time the song appears in the film version, we're already neck-deep in the bowdlerized story, which now is nothing more than the typical "teens put on a show" trope, before the song makes its appearance. It is sung there mostly by two lesser characters—though Judy Garland's Patsy does get to sing one line to her besotted costar.

Rooney is accompanied by an orchestra made up entirely of somber children sawing away at what looks like a hundred violins.

But in the play the song is more than just a soppy serving of sorghum. Billie and Valentine, who don't even exist in the film version, use the song to foreshorten the time between first meeting and first kiss. The dreamy ode to lovers tumbling through time to find each other again makes that inaugural embrace seem more like destiny than mere carnal momentum.

The swirling dreamlike quality of Rodgers's tune gives the listener a feeling of time as mysterious and complex as anything by Stephen Hawking. And Hart's lyrics ride that ethereal melody, allowing the singer to be lost in reverie, confronting a lover like an apparition.

And for a man like Lorenz Hart, standing barely five feet tall, who disparaged his own looks so much it veered toward self-loathing, the thought of reincarnation—star-crossed romance playing out in different times and in different flesh—must have seemed very attractive.

The transformed version of *Babes in Arms* was a huge success at the box office and received two Academy Awards, one for nineteen-year-old lead Mickey Rooney. It's interesting to note that after working so hard to make the script less offensive, the big musical finale features Oscar-winner Rooney along with Judy Garland slapping on the blackface and mugging incessantly through a simulacrum of a traditional minstrel show, with Rooney portraying Mr. Bones, Garland portraying Mr. Tambo, and Douglas McPhail portraying the straight-man interlocutor. All three characters were minstrel show mainstays, which explains but does not excuse their presence.

The performance is at least as one-dimensionally stereotyped as Mickey's cringeworthy portrayal of Mr. Yunioshi in *Breakfast at Tiffany's* twenty-two years later.

Dion DiMucci evolved throughout his career, changing outwardly but

maintaining recognizable characteristics across every iteration. Not reincarnation in the strictest sense but an amazing series of rebirths, taking him from an earnest Teenager in Love to a swaggering Wanderer, a soul-searching friend of Abraham, Martin and John to a hard-edged leather-clad king of the urban jungle who was a template for fellow Italo-rocker Bruce Springsteen. Most recently, he has realized one of his early dreams and become some kind of elder legend, a bluesman from another Delta.

Dion's version of "Where or When," a big hit in 1959, shines a light on the talent behind those transformations. A breathtaking bit of vocal harmony, it was the Belmonts' biggest hit on the *Billboard* charts, beating even the aforementioned "A Teenager in Love." And when Dion's voice bursts through for a solo moment in the bridge, it captures that moment of shimmering persistence of memory in a way the printed word can only hint at.

But so it is with music, it is of a time but also timeless; a thing with which to make memories and the memory itself. Though we seldom consider it, music is built in time as surely as a sculptor or welder works in physical space. Music transcends time by living within it, just as reincarnation allows us to transcend life by living it again and again.

Archival research and clearance: Parker Fishel & David Beal.

Front jacket by Bruce Perry/*The Sydney Morning Herald*/Fairfax Media via Getty Images; pp. v, 28, 175, 185 by Pictorial Press Ltd/Alamy Stock Photo; pp. vi, 39, 48, 83, 93, 224, 248, 258, 330 by Michael Ochs Archives via Getty Images; p. viii by Leonard McCombe/The LIFE Picture Collection/Shutterstock; pp. x–xi, 107, 318, 335, 340 courtesy of Sony Music Entertainment; p. xii by Lynd Ward; p. 3 by Süeddeutsche Zeitung Photo/Alamy Stock Photo; p. 4 © Raeanne Rubenstein, courtesy of the Country Music Hall of Fame and Museum; p. 14 by Coppo di Marcovaldo, image: Alamy Stock Photo; p. 18 *Beggars Banquet* photograph by Michael Josephs © ABKCO Music & Records, Inc. https://www.abkco.com/store/beggars-banquet/; p. 19 Everett Collection, Inc./Alamy Stock Photo; p. 20 by Hulton Archive via Getty Images; p. 26 by © Jean Gaumy/Magnum Photos; p. 30 by Paul Cézanne, image: FineArt/Alamy Stock Photo; p. 31 by Harry Hammond/V&A Images via Getty Images; p. 32 by SuperStock; p. 36 Cover illustration by Robert Osborn. Cover treatment from the pages of *LIFE* © 1962 Meredith Operations Corporation. All rights reserved. Cover treatment reprinted/translated from *LIFE* and published with permission of Meredith Operations Corporation. Reproduction in any manner in any language in whole or in part without written permission is prohibited. *LIFE* and the *LIFE* logo are registered trademarks of Meredith Operations Corporation. Used under license.; p. 38 courtesy of NYC Municipal Archives; pp. 40, 145 courtesy of Universal Music Group; p. 54 by The Protected Art Archive/Alamy Stock Photo; p. 57 by Ernesto Garcia Cabral; p. 58 by Jeremy Woodhouse/PixelChrome; p. 60 by Aaron Rapoport/Corbis via Getty Images; p. 64 by *Los Angeles Examiner*/USC Libraries/Corbis via Getty Images; p. 72 by Lieutenant Whitman, courtesy of the Library of Congress; p. 74 by Basil Wolverton; p. 84 by Rockwell Kent, rights courtesy of Plattsburgh State Art Museum, State University of New York, USA, Rockwell Kent Collection, Bequest of Sally Kent Gorton. All rights reserved.; p. 86 by William James Linton, image: Asar Studios/Alamy Stock Photo; p. 88 by John Springer Collection/Corbis via Getty Images; p. 90 Genaro Molina/*Los Angeles Times*/Contour via Getty Images; pp. 94, 146 by GAB Archive/Redferns via Getty Images; p. 98 © George Rodger/Magnum Photos; p. 103 by Graphic House/Archive Photos via Getty Images; p. 104 by Keystone-France/Gamma-Keystone via Getty Images; p. 110 by Buyenlarge via Getty Images; p. 112 courtesy of Foster Hall Collection, CAM.FHC.2011.01, Center for American Music, University of Pittsburgh; p. 114 by Maureen Light Photography via Getty Images; p. 115 by North Wind Picture Archives/Alamy Stock Photo; p. 116 by PictureLux/The Hollywood Archive/Alamy Stock Photo; p. 119 by Richard Walter/Gamma-Rapho via Getty Images; p. 120 logo courtesy of Brian D. Perskin & Associates, image by Parker Fishel; p. 124 by Orlando/Three Lions via Getty Images; p. 125 by Gilles Petard/Redferns via Getty Images; pp. 126, 133, 149, 282, 284, 307 by Bettmann via Getty Images; p. 128 by Larry Downing/Reuters/Alamy Stock Photo; p. 129 courtesy of the Central Intelligence Agency; p. 130 by Maxim Ersov/Alamy Stock Photo; p. 134 (top) by Warner Brothers/Alamy Stock Photo; p. 134 (bottom) by Photo 12/Alamy Stock Photo; p. 136 by Herb Greene; p. 139 (top) used by permission of Grove Atlantic; p. 139 (bottom) courtesy of Warner